Third Edition

The MixMax Company

HILLEL M. MAXIMON
GEORGE H. SORTER
New York University

McGRAW-HILL PUBLISHING COMPANY

New York St. Louis San Francisco Auckland Bogotá Caracas
Hamburg Lisbon London Madrid Mexico Milan Montreal
New Delhi Oklahoma City Paris San Juan São Paulo Singapore
Sydney Tokyo Toronto

THE MIXMAX COMPANY

1 2 3 4 5 6 7 8 9 0 SEM SEM 8 9 4 3 2 1 0 9

ISBN 0-07-041007-0

The editors were Robert D. Lynch and Johanna Schmid;
the production supervisor was Friederich W. Schulte.
Semline, Inc., was printer and binder.

This book is dedicated to
Shalom Maximon and
Jonathan Maximon.

Contents

Preface

The MixMax Company is a merchandising firm. The company issues annual statements at calendar year-end, December 31, prepared in conformity with generally accepted accounting principles (GAAP). In addition, it prepared interim (monthly and quarterly) financial statements for internal purposes only.

The objectives of this problem-set are to demonstrate transactional analysis (also called the events approach); to develop the mechanics of accounting and financing techniques; and to demonstrate the effects of these techniques on financial statements.

This problem-set contains 18 problems. The first six introduce the relationship between accounting events and financial statements. The next four stress the operating events: bad debt expense, cost of goods sold, depreciation expense, and income taxes. The following four problems focus on the financing events: long-term borrowing, bonds, and stock issues; and the last four cover investing events: leases, and investments in other firms.

Each problem builds on the previous one—always introducing new material and repeating familiar topics. You should **not** refer to previous (or future) problems in order to solve a particular problem. Each problem is self-contained and can be solved independently of any other problem.

In addition to the problem-set, there are three appendices and worksheets. The first appendix is a detailed explanation of transactional analysis. It should be studied thoroughly in order to develop the technique of solving MixMax-type problems.

The second appendix is a summary review of accounts and events. Its purposes are to show the relationship between accounting events, the accounts they affect, and the resultant financial statements, and to assist you in solving the problems in this book.

The third appendix consists of compound interest tables. These tables are used in calculating the effects of alternative debt financing techniques: loans, bonds, and leases.

Worksheets have been provided on which you can work each problem out.

To the Instructor

The MixMax Company, Third Edition is an integrated problem-set for an introductory concepts course in financial accounting. It can be used in conjunction with any accounting textbook if the following topics are taught in sequential order: financial statements (the balance sheet, the income statement, and the statement of cash flows); operating events (bad debt expense, cost of goods sold, depreciation expense, and income taxes); financing events (long-term borrowing, bonds, and common stock); investing events (leases, and investments in other firms).

Like most current accounting textbooks, the third edition of *The MixMax Company* problem-set offers challenging exercises and problems that demonstrate the practical effects of alternative accounting techniques. Unlike most books, this practice-set contains problems that demonstrate transactional analysis, sometimes called the **events approach to accounting.**[1] Transactional analysis is a technique used to disaggregate financial statements into accounting events in order to give users of financial statements new insights into the activities of a firm.

Though the additional exercises and transactional analysis problems can be solved independently, they can be integrated to demonstrate the effects of alternative accounting and financing techniques on financial statements.

The MixMax Company, Third Edition develops on a monthly basis. Each problem introduces new material and reiterates the topics covered in the preceding problems, thus enabling students to strengthen and sharpen their problem-solving skills. Although the problem-set builds from month to month, each problem is independent of any other. Therefore it is neither necessary nor advisable to refer to previous (or future) problems to achieve optimal results.

This book has been tested in different classroom settings. Students and instructors have found these exercises and problems to be challenging and rigorous, yet rewarding and fun. Some have even found them to be addictive, but not injurious to their health!

[1]George H. Sorter, Monroe J. Ingberman, and Hillel M. Maximon, *Financial Accounting: An Events and Cash Flow Approach,* McGraw-Hill, New York, 1990.

Acknowledgments

We are indebted to many people who have contributed to the success of this book. Collectively, to our families for their continued encouragement, and the many students for their constructive feedback.

Individually, we are grateful to our friends: Leonard Harlan, David Kaplan, Stephanie Lovett, and Earl Ludman; to our colleagues at New York University: Norman Berman, John Bildersee, John Cheh, Haim Dov Fried, Patricia McQueen, Michael Schiff, Ashwinpaul Sondhi, Robert Widman; and to Rohit Jain of Temple University, Marilyn Neimark of Baruch College, and Dan Palmon of Rutgers University; whose comments have enriched this book.

Special thanks to Kathleen McGahran and Gordon Shillinglaw of Columbia University for their insightful analysis and review of this problem-set, and to William Vatter who created the prototype of these problems.

Hillel M. Maximon
George H. Sorter

The MixMax Company

The MixMax Company
November 19X0

The following events occurred during the month of November 19X0, relating to The MixMax Company (the company), a merchandising concern:

1. The company hired an accountant to provide accounting and financial planning services. The accountant will begin on January 1, 19X1, and the annual fee is $1,200.
2. 13,000 shares of common stock (par $1) were issued for $13,000.
3. Customers advanced the company $1,700 for future orders.
4. Inventory was purchased on account in the amount of $5,000.
5. The company ordered $2,500 worth of merchandise from a supplier, to be paid when the goods are received.
6. Payments to suppliers of merchandise amounted to $4,000.
7. A customer ordered $1,500 of merchandise, payable when delivered at the end of January 19X1.
8. In addition to the other advances from customers, one customer deposited $300 in advance on a $3,000 order.
9. The company prepaid seven months' rent in the amount of $3,500.
10. The articles of incorporation call for the company to donate to The GimMe, GetMe, DooMe, BuyMe Fund, a non-profit charitable organization.

Required:

a. Determine if the events listed above are accounting events.

b. For each accounting event, indicate if the accounts affected are Assets, Liabilities, or Owners' Equities.

c. For each accounting event, indicate the **titles** of the accounts affected.

d. Record the effect of each accounting event on the equation: Assets = Liabilities + Owners' Equities.

Example: Issue of Common Stock

Assets	=	Liabilities	+	Owners' Equities
+ 13,000	=			+ 13,000

e. Write the journal entry for each accounting event.

f. Repeat part d using T-accounts.

The MixMax Company
Balance Sheet
December 1, 19X0

Assets	12/1/X0
Cash	$ 7,500
Inventory	5,000
Prepaid Rent	3,500
Total Assets	$ 16,000

Liabilities and Owners' Equities	
Advances from Customers	$ 2,000
Accounts Payable Merchandise	1,000
Common Stock	13,000
Total Liabilities and Owners' Equities	$ 16,000

Events occurring during December 19X0

1. Sales during the month were $12,000. Of these, $2,600 were for cash, $7,300 were on credit, and $2,100 were to customers that paid in advance.
2. Operating expenses (exclusive of rent) were $2,500.
3. Advances received from customers during the month were $1,500.
4. Credit purchase of inventory was $8,000.
5. Collections from credit customers were $5,700.
6. Taxes, accrued and paid during the month, were $1,200.
7. Payments to suppliers of services rendered were $2,300.
8. Cost of goods sold was $6,000.
9. Payments to suppliers of merchandise were $5,400.
10. Rent expense was $500.

Required:

From the December 1, 19X0 balance sheet and the events that occurred during the month of December 19X0

a. Prepare a balance sheet as of December 31, 19X0.

b. Prepare an income statement for December 19X0.

c. Prepare a statement of cash receipts and disbursements for December 19X0.

The MixMax Company
Comparative Balance Sheets
January 1, 19X1 and January 31, 19X1

Assets	1/1/X1	1/31/X1
Cash	$ 8,400	$ 11,000
Accounts Receivable	1,600	7,600
Inventory	7,000	10,000
Prepaid Rent	3,000	2,500
Property, Plant and Equipment	0	45,000
Accumulated Depreciation	0	(675)
Total Assets	$ 20,000	$ 75,425

Liabilities and Owners' Equities		
Advances from Customers	$ 1,400	$ 800
Accounts Payable Merchandise	3,600	5,100
Accounts Payable Services	200	1,275
Interest Payable	0	450
Taxes Payable	0	3,200
Current Portion of Debt	0	6,373
Long-Term Debt	0	38,627
Common Stock [see note]	13,000	13,000
Retained Earnings	1,800	6,600
Total Liabilities and Owners' Equities	$ 20,000	$ 75,425

Note:

The MixMax Company did not issue common stock during January 19X1.

The MixMax Company
January 19X1
T-Accounts

Alternative
to the Income Summary:
Individual Income Accounts

Income Summary

Retained Earnings

Common Stock

Cash

Accounts Receivable

Inventory

Prepaid Rent

Accumulated Depreciation

Property, Plant and Equipment

The MixMax Company
January 19X1
T-Accounts

Current Portion of Debt

Advances from Customers

Accounts Payable Merchandise

Accounts Payable Services

Interest Payable

Long-Term Debt

Taxes Payable

The MixMax Company
Statement of Cash Receipts and Disbursements
January 19X1

Cash Receipts	
Collections from Credit Customers	$ 20,500
Advances from Customers	2,900
Total Cash Receipts	$ 23,400
Cash Disbursements	
Payments to Suppliers of Merchandise	$ 16,500
Payments to Suppliers of Services	4,300
Total Cash Disbursements	$ 20,800
Excess Cash Receipts over Cash Disbursements	$ 2,600

===

Thought Question

Although the balances in Property, Plant and Equipment, and Long-Term Debt increased, there was neither a cash disbursement for the purchase of property, plant and equipment, nor a cash receipt for long-term borrowing, in the statement of cash receipts and disbursements. Why?

===

Required:

a. List all of the events that occurred during January 19X1. Refer to Appendix 1 for a method of solving this problem.

b. Prepare an income statement for January 19X1.

The MixMax Company
Comparative Balance Sheets
February 1, 19X1 and February 29, 19X1

Assets	2/1/X1	2/29/X1
Cash	$ 11,000	$ 23,000
Accounts Receivable	7,600	17,000
Inventory	10,000	5,000
Prepaid Rent	2,500	2,000
Property, Plant and Equipment	45,000	45,000
Accumulated Depreciation	(675)	(1,350)
Total Assets	$ 75,425	$ 90,650

Liabilities and Owners' Equities		
Advances from Customers	$ 800	$ 0
Accounts Payable Merchandise	5,100	4,000
Accounts Payable Services	1,275	3,456
Interest Payable	450	445
Taxes Payable	3,200	9,400
Current Portion of Debt	6,373	5,822
Long-Term Debt	38,627	38,627
Common Stock	13,000	13,000
Retained Earnings	6,600	15,900
Total Liabilities and Owners' Equities	$ 75,425	$ 90,650

==

Thought Question

Why did the balance in the Long-Term Debt account not decrease?

==

Alternative
to the Income Summary:
Individual Income Accounts

The MixMax Company
February 19X1
T-Accounts

Income Summary

Retained Earnings

Common Stock

Cash

Accounts Receivable

Inventory

Prepaid Rent

Accumulated Depreciation

Property, Plant and Equipment

The MixMax Company
February 19X1
T-Accounts

Current Portion of Debt

Advances from Customers

Accounts Payable Merchandise

Accounts Payable Services

Interest Payable

Long-Term Debt

Taxes Payable

The MixMax Company
Income Statement
February 19X1

Revenues		
Sales Revenue		$ 48,000
Total Revenues		$ 48,000
Expenses		
Cost of Goods Sold	$ 21,000	
Operating Expenses	9,880	
Depreciation Expense	675	
Rent Expense	500	
Interest Expense	445	
Tax Expense	6,200	
Total Expenses	$ 38,700	(38,700)
Net Income		$ 9,300

==

Thought Questions

For what accounting event would you debit (decrease) the account Advances from Customers?

What is the **minimum** that the account Advances from Customers could have been debited for during the month of February?

What is the **maximum** that the account Advances from Customers could have been debited for during the month of February?

==

Required:

a. List all of the events that occurred during February 19X1.

b. Prepare a statement of cash receipts and disbursements for February 19X1. This assignment is the reverse of that in January 19X1. In January, you were given comparative balance sheets and a statement of cash receipts and disbursements, and were asked to prepare an income statement. In this problem, you are given comparative balance sheets and an income statement, and are asked to prepare a statement of cash receipts and disbursements.

This page was left blank intentionally.

Alternative
to the Income Summary:
Individual Income Accounts

The MixMax Company
March 19X1
T-Accounts

Income Summary

Retained Earnings

Common Stock

Cash

Accounts Receivable

Inventory

Prepaid Rent

Accumulated Depreciation

Property,
Plant and Equipment

The MixMax Company
March 19X1
T-Accounts

Current Portion of Debt

Accounts Payable
Merchandise

Accounts Payable
Services

Interest Payable

Long-Term Debt

Taxes Payable

The MixMax Company
Post-Closing Trial Balance Sheet as of March 1, 19X1
Pre-Closing Trial Balance Sheet as of March 31, 19X1

Debit Balance Accounts	3/1/X1	3/31/X1
Cash	$ 23,000	$ 18,400
Accounts Receivable	17,000	24,000
Inventory	5,000	5,000
Prepaid Rent	2,000	1,500
Property, Plant and Equipment	45,000	45,000
Cost of Goods Sold	-	20,000
Operating Expenses	-	8,386
Depreciation Expense	-	675
Rent Expense	-	500
Interest Expense	-	439
Tax Expense	-	4,000
Total Debit Balances	$ 92,000	$ 127,900

Credit Balance Accounts		
Accumulated Depreciation	$ 1,350	$ 2,025
Accounts Payable Merchandise	4,000	9,000
Accounts Payable Services	3,456	4,943
Interest Payable	445	439
Taxes Payable	9,400	0
Current Portion of Debt	5,822	5,266
Long-Term Debt	38,627	38,627
Common Stock	13,000	13,000
Retained Earnings	15,900	14,600
Sales Revenue	-	40,000
Total Credit Balances	$ 92,000	$ 127,900

==

Thought Question

What caused the Retained Earnings account to decrease by $1,300?

==

Required:

a. List all of the events that occurred during March 19X1.

b. Prepare a statement of cash receipts and disbursements for March 19X1.

The MixMax Company
Comparative Balance Sheets
January 1, 19X1 and March 31, 19X1

Assets	1/1/X1	3/31/X1
Cash	$ 8,400	$ 18,400
Accounts Receivable	1,600	24,000
Inventory	7,000	5,000
Prepaid Rent	3,000	1,500
Property, Plant and Equipment	0	45,000
Accumulated Depreciation	0	(2,025)
Total Assets	$ 20,000	$ 91,875

Liabilities and Owners' Equities		
Advances from Customers	$ 1,400	$ 0
Accounts Payable Merchandise	3,600	9,000
Accounts Payable Services	200	4,943
Interest Payable	0	439
Current Portion of Debt	0	5,266
Long-Term Debt	0	38,627
Common Stock	13,000	13,000
Retained Earnings	1,800	20,600
Total Liabilities and Owners' Equities	$ 20,000	$ 91,875

Thought Questions

Can you determine the original amount of borrowing solely from the accompanying financial statements?

Could events impacting the comparative balance sheets have warranted a different presentation of the statement of cash flows?

What events require the preparation of the schedule of significant noncash financing **and** investing events?

The MixMax Company
First Quarter 19X1
T-Accounts

Alternative to the Income Summary: Individual Income Accounts

Income Summary

Retained Earnings

Dividends Payable

Common Stock

Cash

CfO

Financing

Investing

Indirect Method of Calculating Cash from Operations

NI

CfO

Accounts Receivable

Inventory

Prepaid Rent

Accumulated Depreciation

Property, Plant and Equipment

The MixMax Company
First Quarter 19X1
T-Accounts

Current Portion of Debt

Advances from Customers

Accounts Payable Merchandise

Accounts Payable Services

Interest Payable

Long-Term Debt

Taxes Payable

The MixMax Company
Reconciliation of Income Events to Operating Cash Flow Events
First Quarter 19X1

	Income Events	Events not associated with Operating Cash Flows	(Debit) Credit Change in Current Operating Account(s)	**Operating Cash Flow Events**
Sales Revenue				
Sales Revenue not associated with Cash Flows from Operations				
Decrease (Increase) in Accounts Receivable				
Increase (Decrease) in Advances from Customers				
Collections from Customers				
Cost of Goods Sold				
Cost of Goods Sold not associated with Cash Flows from Operations				
Decrease (Increase) in Inventory				
Increase (Decrease) in Accounts Payable Merchandise				
Payments to Suppliers of Merchandise				
Operating Expenses				
Operating Expenses not associated with Cash Flows from Operations				
Increase (Decrease) in Accounts Payable Services				
Payments to Suppliers of Services				
Depreciation Expense				
Depreciation Expense not associated with Cash Flows from Operations				
No Current Operating Accounts affected				
Operating Cash Flows associated with Depreciation				
Rent Expense				
Rent Expense not associated with Cash Flows from Operations				
Decrease (Increase) in Prepaid Rent				
Payment of Rent				
Interest Expense				
Interest Expense not associated with Cash Flows from Operations				
Increase (Decrease) in Interest Payable				
Interest Payment				
Tax Expense				
Tax Expense not associated with Cash Flows from Operations				
Increase (Decrease) in Taxes Payable				
Tax Payment				
Net Income				
Total Income Events not associated with Cash Flows from Operations				
Decrease (Increase) in Net Current Operating Accounts				
Cash Flows from Operating Events				

The MixMax Company
Income Statement
First Quarter 19X1

Revenues		
Sales Revenue		$ 118,000
Total Revenues		$ 118,000
Expenses		
Cost of Goods Sold	$ 56,000	
Operating Expense	23,641	
Depreciation Expense	2,025	
Rent Expense	1,500	
Interest Expense	1,334	
Tax Expense	13,400	
Total Expenses	$ 97,900	(97,900)
Net Income		$ 20,100

Statement of Cash Flows
First Quarter 19X1

Cash Inflows from Operating Events		$ 12,407
Cash Flows from Financing Events		
Total Financing Events	$?	?
Cash Flows from Investing Events		
Total Investing Events	$?	?
Increase in Cash		$ 10,000

Required:

a. List all of the events that occurred during the first quarter of 19X1.

b. The accountant for The MixMax Company ran out of ink (and steam) in preparing the statement of cash flows for the first quarter of 19X1. From the accompanying comparative balance sheets and related income statement, complete the statement for the company. (In answering this question, consider the **Thought Questions** on page 10.)

The MixMax Company
Comparative Balance Sheets
April 1, 19X1 and April 30, 19X1

Assets	4/1/X1	4/30/X1
Cash	$ 18,400	$ 35,700
Accounts Receivable	24,000	40,000
Allowance for Doubtful Accounts	0	(?)
Inventory	5,000	3,000
Prepaid Rent	1,500	1,000
Property, Plant and Equipment	45,000	45,000
Accumulated Depreciation	(2,025)	(2,700)
Total Assets	$ 91,875	$?

Liabilities and Owners' Equities		
Accounts Payable Merchandise	$ 9,000	$ 8,000
Accounts Payable Services	4,943	4,636
Interest Payable	439	433
Taxes Payable	0	12,000
Current Portion of Debt	5,266	4,704
Long-Term Debt	38,627	38,627
Common Stock	13,000	13,000
Retained Earnings	20,600	38,600
Total Liabilities and Owners' Equities	$ 91,875	$ 120,000

Notes:

1. At the end of the month, but before preparing its financial statements, The MixMax Company was notified by the attorney of one of its credit customers that the customer had filed for bankruptcy during the month of April 19X1, and would not pay $600 in bills. The accountant realized that no provision had been made for such eventualities.

   You are asked to assist the accountant in comparing the effects of alternative accounting methods used to make provisions for such occurrences. The alternatives are: the percentage-of-sales method (with the estimate of uncollectibility of 4 percent of current credit sales), or the aging-of-receivables method calculated from the aging schedule presented below. Credit sales were $65,000 during the month of April.

Age of Accounts	Balance in Accounts	Estimate of Uncollectibility
0 - 30 days	$ 26,000	1%
31 - 60 days	9,000	5%
61 - 90 days	4,000	15%
> 90 days	1,000	69%

2. Depreciation and rent expenses are included in operating expenses.

The MixMax Company
April 19X1
T-Accounts

Alternative
to the Income Summary:
Individual Income Accounts

Income Summary

Retained Earnings

Common Stock

Cash

CfO

Financing

Investing

Indirect Method
of Calculating
Cash from Operations

NI

CfO

Allowance for Doubtful Accounts

Accounts Receivable

Inventory

Prepaid Rent

Accumulated Depreciation

Property,
Plant and Equipment

The MixMax Company
April 19X1
T-Accounts

Current Portion of Debt

Accounts Payable Merchandise

Accounts Payable Services

Interest Payable

Long-Term Debt

Taxes Payable

The MixMax Company
Reconciliation of Income Events to Operating Cash Flow Events
April 19X1

	Income Events	Events not associated with Operating Cash Flows	(Debit) Credit Change in Current Operating Account(s)	**Operating Cash Flow Events**
Sales Revenue				
less: **Bad Debt Expense**				
Net Sales Revenue				
Sales Revenue not associated with Cash Flows from Operations				
Decrease (Increase) in Accounts Receivable				
Increase (Decrease) in Allowance for Doubtful Accounts				
Collections from Customers				
Cost of Goods Sold				
Cost of Goods Sold not associated with Cash Flows from Operations				
Decrease (Increase) in Inventory				
Increase (Decrease) in Accounts Payable Merchandise				
Payments to Suppliers of Merchandise				
Operating Expenses				
Operating Expenses not associated with Cash Flows from Operations				
Decrease (Increase) in Prepaid Rent				
Increase (Decrease) in Accounts Payable Services				
Payments to Suppliers of Services				
Interest Expense				
Interest Expense not associated with Cash Flows from Operations				
Increase (Decrease) in Interest Payable				
Interest Payment				
Tax Expense				
Tax Expense not associated with Cash Flows from Operations				
Increase (Decrease) in Taxes Payable				
Tax Payment				
Net Income				
Total Income Events not associated with Cash Flows from Operations				
Decrease (Increase) in Net Current Operating Accounts				
Cash Flows from Operating Events				

The MixMax Company
Income Statement
April 19X1

Revenues		
Sales Revenue [see note 1]		$ 77,000
Bad Debt Expense [see note 1]		(?)
Net Sales Revenue		$?
Total Revenues		$?
Expenses		
Cost of Goods Sold	$ 32,000	
Operating Expenses [see note 2]	11,967	
Interest Expense	433	
Tax Expense	12,000	
Total Expenses	$ 56,400	(56,400)
Net Income		$ 18,000

Statement of Cash Flows
April 19X1

Cash Inflows from Operating Events		$ 17,862
Cash (Outflows) from Financing Events		
Repayment of Loan	$ (562)	
Total Financing Events	$ (562)	(562)
Increase in Cash		$ 17,300

Required:

a. List all of the events that occurred during April 19X1.

b. Fill in all of the question (?) marks.

The MixMax Company
Comparative Balance Sheets
May 1, 19X1 and May 31, 19X1

Assets	5/1/X1	5/31/X1
Cash	$ 35,700	$ 47,975
Accounts Receivable	40,000	59,000
Allowance for Doubtful Accounts	(2,000)	(4,100)
Inventory	3,000	8,000
Prepaid Rent	1,000	500
Property, Plant and Equipment	45,000	45,000
Accumulated Depreciation	(2,700)	(3,375)
Total Assets	$ 120,000	$ 153,000

Liabilities and Owners' Equities	5/1/X1	5/31/X1
Accounts Payable Merchandise	$ 8,000	$ 11,000
Accounts Payable Services	4,636	4,209
Interest Payable	433	428
Taxes Payable	12,000	24,400
Current Portion of Debt	4,704	4,136
Long-Term Debt	38,627	38,627
Common Stock	13,000	13,000
Retained Earnings	38,600	57,200
Total Liabilities and Owners' Equities	$ 120,000	$ 153,000

The MixMax Company
May 19X1
T-Accounts

Alternative to the Income Summary: Individual Income Accounts

Income Summary

Retained Earnings

Common Stock

Cash

CfO

Financing

Investing

Indirect Method of Calculating Cash from Operations

NI

CfO

Allowance for Doubtful Accounts

Accounts Receivable

Inventory

Prepaid Rent

Accumulated Depreciation

Property, Plant and Equipment

The MixMax Company
May 19X1
T-Accounts

Current Portion of Debt

Accounts Payable Merchandise

Accounts Payable Services

Interest Payable

Long-Term Debt

Taxes Payable

The MixMax Company
Reconciliation of Income Events to Operating Cash Flow Events
May 19X1

	Income Events	Events not associated with Operating Cash Flows	(Debit) Credit Change in Current Operating Account(s)	**Operating Cash Flow Events**
Sales Revenue				
less: **Bad Debt Expense**				
Net Sales Revenue				
Sales Revenue not associated with Cash Flows from Operations				
Decrease (Increase) in Accounts Receivable				
Increase (Decrease) in Allowance for Doubtful Accounts				
Collections from Customers				
Cost of Goods Sold				
Cost of Goods Sold not associated with Cash Flows from Operations				
Decrease (Increase) in Inventory				
Increase (Decrease) in Accounts Payable Merchandise				
Payments to Suppliers of Merchandise				
Operating Expenses				
Operating Expenses not associated with Cash Flows from Operations				
Decrease (Increase) in Prepaid Rent				
Increase (Decrease) in Accounts Payable Services				
Payments to Suppliers of Services				
Interest Expense				
Interest Expense not associated with Cash Flows from Operations				
Increase (Decrease) in Interest Payable				
Interest Payment				
Tax Expense				
Tax Expense not associated with Cash Flows from Operations				
Increase (Decrease) in Taxes Payable				
Tax Payment				
Net Income				
Total Income Events not associated with Cash Flows from Operations				
Decrease (Increase) in Net Current Operating Accounts				
Cash Flows from Operating Events				

The MixMax Company
Income Statement
May 19X1

Revenues		
Sales Revenue		$ 77,000
Bad Debt Expense		(2,480)
Net Sales Revenue		$ 74,520
Total Revenues		$ 74,520
Expenses		
Cost of Goods Sold	$ 35,000	
Operating Expenses	8,092	
Interest Expense	428	
Tax Expense	12,400	
Total Expenses	$ 55,920	(55,920)
Net Income		$ 18,600

Statement of Cash Flows
May 19X1

Cash Inflows from Operating Events		$?
Cash (Outflows) from Financing Events		
Repayment of Loan	$ (568)	
Total Financing Events	$ (568)	(568)
Increase in Cash		$?

Required:

a. List all of the events that occurred during May 19X1.

b. Fill in all of the question (?) marks.

Additional Exercises: Independent of the problem above.

Complete the schedules on pages 16 and 17.

From the schedule of purchases and sales of merchandise below, calculate Cost of Goods Sold from the beginning of November 19X0 through, and including, the end of May 19X1 using the following flow assumptions: FIFO and LIFO periodic; FIFO and LIFO perpetual; and average cost.

Period	---Purchases---- Unit Cost	Total Cost	------Sales------ Unit Price	Total Price
Nov X0	$ 1.00	$ 5,000	$ 0	$ 0
Dec X0	2.00	8,000	4.00	12,000
Jan X1	3.00	18,000	6.00	30,000
Feb X1	4.00	16,000	8.00	48,000
Mar X1	5.00	20,000	10.00	40,000
Apr X1	6.00	30,000	11.00	77,000
May X1	5.00	40,000	11.00	77,000

Schedule of Purchases and Sales

Period	--------Purchases----------- Unit Cost	Total Purchases	Units Purchased	------------Sales----------- Unit Price	Total Sales	Units Sold
Nov X0	_____	_____	_____	_____	_____	_____
Dec X0	_____	_____	_____	_____	_____	_____
Jan X1	_____	_____	_____	_____	_____	_____
Feb X1	_____	_____	_____	_____	_____	_____
Mar X1	_____	_____	_____	_____	_____	_____
Apr X1	_____	_____	_____	_____	_____	_____
May X1	_____	_____	_____	_____	_____	_____

Inventory Schedule assuming FIFO Periodic Flow

Period	Beginning Balance	Purchases	Ending Balance	Cost of Goods Sold
Nov to May	0	_____	_____	_____

Inventory Schedule assuming LIFO Periodic Flow

Period	Beginning Balance	Purchases	Ending Balance	Cost of Goods Sold
Nov X0	0	_____	_____	_____

Inventory Schedule assuming FIFO Perpetual Flow

Period	Beginning Balance	Purchases	Ending Balance	Cost of Goods Sold
Nov X0	0			
Dec X0				
Jan X1				
Feb X1				
Mar X1				
Apr X1				
May X1				

Inventory Schedule assuming LIFO Perpetual Flow

Period	Beginning Balance	Purchases	Ending Balance	Cost of Goods Sold
Nov X0	0			
Dec X0				
Jan X1				
Feb X1				
Mar X1				
Apr X1				
May X1				

Inventory Schedule assuming Average Cost Flow

Period	Beginning Balance	Purchases	Ending Balance	Cost of Goods Sold
Nov X0	0			
Dec X0				
Jan X1				
Feb X1				
Mar X1				
Apr X1				
May X1				

The MixMax Company
Comparative Balance Sheets
June 1, 19X1 and June 30, 19X1

Assets	6/1/X1	6/30/X1
Cash	$ 47,975	$?
Accounts Receivable	59,000	63,000
Allowance for Doubtful Accounts	(4,100)	(5,600)
Inventory	8,000	14,000
Prepaid Rent	500	0
Property, Plant and Equipment [see notes]	45,000	27,000
Accumulated Depreciation [see notes]	(3,375)	(?)
Total Assets	$ 153,000	$?

Liabilities and Owners' Equities		
Accounts Payable Merchandise	$ 11,000	$ 14,500
Accounts Payable Services	4,209	7,760
Interest Payable	428	422
Taxes Payable	24,400	0
Current Portion of Debt	4,136	3,563
Deferred Taxes	0	198
Long-Term Debt	38,627	38,627
Common Stock	13,000	13,000
Retained Earnings	57,200	61,900
Total Liabilities and Owners' Equities	$ 153,000	$ 139,970

Notes:

1. Recall (from the January 19X1 financial statements) that The MixMax Company purchased equipment on January 1, 19X1, in the amount of $45,000. The expected life for all of the equipment is 5 years. Below is a schedule relating to the equipment purchased:

Unit	Cost	Salvage Value	Market Value (as of 6/30/X1)
Truck	$ 18,000	$ 1,800	$ 16,000
Wagon	14,400	1,440	14,000
Auto	12,600	1,260	12,900
Totals	$ 45,000	$ 4,500	$ 42,900

2. The company sold its truck at the end of June.

===

Thought Question

Suppose that The MixMax Company sold the auto on June 30 for $12,000. What effect would the sale have had on its June financial statements?

===

The MixMax Company
June 19X1
T-Accounts

Alternative to the Income Summary: Individual Income Accounts

Income Summary

Retained Earnings

Dividends Payable

Common Stock

Cash

CfO

Financing

Investing

Indirect Method of Calculating Cash from Operations

NI

CfO

Allowance for Doubtful Accounts

Accounts Receivable

Inventory

Prepaid Rent

Accumulated Depreciation

Property, Plant and Equipment

The MixMax Company
June 19X1
T-Accounts

Current Portion of Debt

Accounts Payable Merchandise

Accounts Payable Services

Interest Payable

Long-Term Debt

Taxes Payable

Deferred Taxes

The MixMax Company
Reconciliation of Income Events to Operating Cash Flow Events
June 19X1

	Income Events	Events not associated with Operating Cash Flows	(Debit) Credit Change in Current Operating Account(s)	**Operating Cash Flow Events**
Sales Revenue				
less: **Bad Debt Expense**				
Net Sales Revenue				
Sales Revenue not associated with Cash Flows from Operations				
Decrease (Increase) in Accounts Receivable				
Increase (Decrease) in Allowance for Doubtful Accounts				
Collections from Customers				
Cost of Goods Sold				
Cost of Goods Sold not associated with Cash Flows from Operations				
Decrease (Increase) in Inventory				
Increase (Decrease) in Accounts Payable Merchandise				
Payments to Suppliers of Merchandise				
Operating Expenses				
Operating Expenses not associated with Cash Flows from Operations				
Decrease (Increase) in Prepaid Rent				
Increase (Decrease) in Accounts Payable Services				
Payments to Suppliers of Services				
Interest Expense				
Interest Expense not associated with Cash Flows from Operations				
Increase (Decrease) in Interest Payable				
Interest Payment				
Loss on Sale of Property, Plant and Equipment				
Loss on Sale not associated with Cash Flows from Operations				
No Current Operating Accounts affected				
Operating Cash Flows associated with the Sale				
Tax Expense				
Tax Expense not associated with Cash Flows from Operations				
Increase (Decrease) in Taxes Payable				
Tax Payment				
Net Income				
Total Income Events not associated with Cash Flows from Operations				
Decrease (Increase) in Net Current Operating Accounts				
Cash Flows from Operating Events				

The MixMax Company
Income Statement
June 19X1

Revenues		
Sales Revenue		$ 55,000
Bad Debt Expense		(2,000)
Net Sales Revenue		$ 53,000
Total Revenues		$ 53,000
Expenses and Losses		
Cost of Goods Sold	$ 30,000	
Operating Expenses	12,198	
Interest Expense	422	
Loss on Sale of Property, Plant and Equipment	380	
Tax Expense	4,000	
Total Expenses and Losses	$ 47,000	(47,000)
Net Income		$ 6,000

Statement of Cash Flows
June 19X1

Cash (Outflows) from Operating Events		$ (18,102)
Cash (Outflows) from Financing Events		
Repayment of Loan	$ (573)	
Payment of Dividends	(1,300)	
Total Financing Events	$ (1,873)	(1,873)
Cash Inflows from Investing Events		
Sale of Property, Plant and Equipment	$?	
Total Investing Events	$?	?
(Decrease) in Cash		$ (?)

Required:

a. List all of the events that occurred during June 19X1.

b. Fill in all of the question (?) marks.

Additional Exercises: Independent of the problem above.

Complete the schedules on page 20 and answer the questions on page 21.

a. From the information provided in the schedule below, calculate the **annual** and **monthly** depreciation expense for all of the equipment, assuming an expected useful life of 5 years, using the: straight-line, sum-of-the-years' digits, and double-declining balance methods of depreciation.

Unit	Cost	Salvage Value	Market Value (as of 6/30/X1)
Truck	$ 18,000	$ 1,800	$ 16,000
Wagon	14,400	1,440	14,000
Auto	12,600	1,260	12,900
Totals	$ 45,000	$ 4,500	$ 42,900

Straight-Line Method

Year	Annual Expense	Monthly Expense	Year-End Book Value
19X1	______	______	______
19X2	______	______	______
19X3	______	______	______
19X4	______	______	______
19X5	______	______	______

Sum-of-the-Years' Digits Method

Year	Annual Expense	Monthly Expense	Year-End Book Value
19X1	______	______	______
19X2	______	______	______
19X3	______	______	______
19X4	______	______	______
19X5	______	______	______

Double-Declining Balance Method

Year	Annual Expense	Monthly Expense	Year-End Book Value
19X1	______	______	______
19X2	______	______	______
19X3	______	______	______
19X4	______	______	______
19X5	______	______	______

b. <u>If</u> the company opted on January 1, to depreciate its property, plant and equipment using the double-declining balance method for tax purposes and the straight-line method for financial reporting purposes, what effect(s), if any, would it have had on its January financial statements? Its June financial statements? (Assume a 40 percent tax rate.)

The MixMax Company
Comparative Balance Sheets
April 1, 19X1 and June 30, 19X1

Assets	4/1/X1	6/30/X1
Cash	$ 18,400	$ 44,000
Accounts Receivable	24,000	63,000
Allowance for Doubtful Accounts	0	(5,600)
Inventory	5,000	14,000
Prepaid Rent	1,500	0
Property, Plant and Equipment	45,000	27,000
Accumulated Depreciation	(2,025)	(2,430)
Total Assets	$ 91,875	$ 139,970

Liabilities and Owners' Equities		
Accounts Payable Merchandise	$ 9,000	$ 14,500
Accounts Payable Services	4,943	7,760
Interest Payable	439	422
Current Portion of Debt	5,266	3,563
Deferred Taxes	0	198
Long-Term Debt	38,627	38,627
Common Stock	13,000	13,000
Retained Earnings	20,600	61,900
Total Liabilities and Owners' Equities	$ 91,875	$ 139,970

The MixMax Company
Second Quarter 19X1
T-Accounts

Alternative to the Income Summary: Individual Income Accounts

Income Summary

Retained Earnings

Dividends Payable

Common Stock

Cash

CfO

Financing

Investing

Indirect Method of Calculating Cash from Operations

NI

CfO

Allowance for Doubtful Accounts

Accounts Receivable

Inventory

Prepaid Rent

Accumulated Depreciation

Property, Plant and Equipment

Current Portion of Debt

Accounts Payable Merchandise

Accounts Payable Services

Interest Payable

Long-Term Debt

Taxes Payable

Deferred Taxes

The MixMax Company
Reconciliation of Income Events to Operating Cash Flow Events
Second Quarter 19X1

	Income Events	Events not associated with Operating Cash Flows	(Debit) Credit Change in Current Operating Account(s)	**Operating Cash Flow Events**
Sales Revenue				
less: **Bad Debt Expense**				
Net Sales Revenue				
Sales Revenue not associated with Cash Flows from Operations				
Decrease (Increase) in Accounts Receivable				
Increase (Decrease) in Allowance for Doubtful Accounts				
Collections from Customers				
Cost of Goods Sold				
Cost of Goods Sold not associated with Cash Flows from Operations				
Decrease (Increase) in Inventory				
Increase (Decrease) in Accounts Payable Merchandise				
Payments to Suppliers of Merchandise				
Operating Expenses				
Operating Expenses not associated with Cash Flows from Operations				
Decrease (Increase) in Prepaid Rent				
Increase (Decrease) in Accounts Payable Services				
Payments to Suppliers of Services				
Interest Expense				
Interest Expense not associated with Cash Flows from Operations				
Increase (Decrease) in Interest Payable				
Interest Payment				
Loss on Sale of Property, Plant and Equipment				
Loss on Sale not associated with Cash Flows from Operations				
No Current Operating Accounts affected				
Operating Cash Flows associated with the Sale				
Tax Expense				
Tax Expense not associated with Cash Flows from Operations				
Increase (Decrease) in Taxes Payable				
Tax Payment				
Net Income				
Total Income Events not associated with Cash Flows from Operations				
Decrease (Increase) in Net Current Operating Accounts				
Cash Flows from Operating Events				

The MixMax Company
Income Statement
Second Quarter 19X1

Revenues		
Sales Revenue		$ 209,000
Bad Debt Expense		(7,080)
Net Sales Revenue		$ 201,920
Total Revenues		$ 201,920
Expenses and Losses		
Cost of Goods Sold	$ 97,000	
Operating Expenses	32,257	
Interest Expense	1,283	
Loss on Sale of Property, Plant and Equipment	380	
Tax Expense	28,400	
Total Expenses and Losses	$ 159,320	(159,320)
Net Income		$ 42,600

Statement of Cash Flows
Second Quarter 19X1

Cash Inflows from Operating Events		$ 12,603
Cash (Outflows) from Financing Events		
Repayment of Loan	$ (1,703)	
Payment of Dividend	(1,300)	
Total Financing Events	$ (3,003)	(3,003)
Cash Inflows from Investing Events		
Sale of Property, Plant and Equipment	$ 16,000	
Total Investing Events	$ 16,000	16,000
Increase in Cash		$ 25,600

==

Thought Question

Explain the difference between
Net Income and Cash Flows from Operating Events.

==

Required:

List all of the events that occurred during the second quarter of 19X1.

The MixMax Company
Comparative Balance Sheets
July 1, 19X1 and July 31, 19X1

Assets	7/1/X1	7/31/X1
Cash	$ 44,000	$ 41,000
Accounts Receivable	63,000	67,000
Allowance for Doubtful Accounts	(5,600)	(7,280)
Inventory	14,000	28,000
Property, Plant and Equipment	27,000	27,000
Accumulated Depreciation	(2,430)	(2,835)
Total Assets	$ 139,970	$ 152,885

Liabilities and Owners' Equities		
Accounts Payable Merchandise	$ 14,500	$ 19,000
Accounts Payable Services	7,760	4,260
Interest Payable	422	416
Taxes Payable	0	4,802
Current Portion of Debt	3,563	?
Deferred Taxes	198	396
Long-Term Debt	38,627	38,627
Common Stock	13,000	13,000
Retained Earnings	61,900	?
Total Liabilities and Owners' Equities	$ 139,970	$?

The MixMax Company
July 19X1
T-Accounts

Alternative to the Income Summary: Individual Income Accounts

Income Summary

Retained Earnings

Common Stock

Cash

CfO

Financing

Investing

Indirect Method of Calculating Cash from Operations

NI

CfO

Allowance for Doubtful Accounts

Accounts Receivable

Inventory

Accumulated Depreciation

Property, Plant and Equipment

Current Portion of Debt

Accounts Payable Merchandise

Accounts Payable Services

Interest Payable

Long-Term Debt

Taxes Payable

Deferred Taxes

The MixMax Company
Reconciliation of Income Events to Operating Cash Flow Events
July 19X1

	Income Events	Events not associated with Operating Cash Flows	(Debit) Credit Change in Current Operating Account(s)	**Operating Cash Flow Events**
Sales Revenue				
less: **Bad Debt Expense**				
Net Sales Revenue				
Sales Revenue not associated with Cash Flows from Operations				
Decrease (Increase) in Accounts Receivable				
Increase (Decrease) in Allowance for Doubtful Accounts				
Collections from Customers				
Cost of Goods Sold				
Cost of Goods Sold not associated with Cash Flows from Operations				
Decrease (Increase) in Inventory				
Increase (Decrease) in Accounts Payable Merchandise				
Payments to Suppliers of Merchandise				
Operating Expenses				
Operating Expenses not associated with Cash Flows from Operations				
Increase (Decrease) in Accounts Payable Services				
Payments to Suppliers of Services				
Interest Expense				
Interest Expense not associated with Cash Flows from Operations				
Increase (Decrease) in Interest Payable				
Interest Payment				
Tax Expense				
Tax Expense not associated with Cash Flows from Operations				
Increase (Decrease) in Taxes Payable				
Tax Payment				
Net Income				
Total Income Events not associated with Cash Flows from Operations				
Decrease (Increase) in Net Current Operating Accounts				
Cash Flows from Operating Events				

The MixMax Company
Income Statement
July 19X1

Revenues		
Sales Revenue		$ 72,000
Bad Debt Expense		(2,880)
Net Sales Revenue		$ 69,120
Total Revenues		$ 69,120
Expenses		
Cost of Goods Sold	$ 42,000	
Operating Expenses	14,204	
Interest Expense	416	
Tax Expense	?	
Total Expenses	$?	(?)
Net Income		$?

Statement of Cash Flows
July 19X1

Cash (Outflows) from Operating Events		$ (?)
Cash (Outflows) from Financing Events		
Repayment of Loan	$ (579)	
Total Financing Events	$ (579)	(579)
(Decrease) in Cash		$ (?)

Thought Questions

What is the **minimum** that Tax Expense could be?

Why must the **minimum** Tax Expense be the **actual** Tax Expense?

Required:

a. List all of the events that occurred during July 19X1.

b. Fill in all of the question (?) marks.

Additional Exercises: Independent of the problem above.

Complete the schedules on page 27.

Recall the $45,000 loan that The MixMax Company arranged to finance the purchase of its equipment back on January 1, 19X1.

The terms of the loan required monthly payments of $1,001, the first one to be made on February 1, 19X1, and the last on January 1, 19X6 (5 years), at a 12 percent annual interest rate, compounded monthly.

Using the tables in Appendix 3, complete the schedule for loan **a**.

Alternatively, the company could have borrowed the same $45,000, at the same interest rate (12 percent compounded monthly), for the same number of periods (60), by making one of the following monthly payments:

b. $ 726
c. 450
d. 174

Using the tables in Appendix 3, complete the remaining schedules for loans **b, c,** and **d.**

	Loan (a)	**Loan (b)**	**Loan (c)**	**Loan (d)**
Interest Rate	______	______	______	______
Length of Period	______	______	______	______
Number of Periods	______	______	______	______
First Period's Payment	______	______	______	______
First Period's Expense	______	______	______	______
Total First Year's Payments	______	______	______	______
Total First Year's Expense	______	______	______	______
Total Periodic Payments	______	______	______	______
Final Payment	______	______	______	______
Total Payments	______	______	______	______
Present Value of Total Payments	______	______	______	______
Total Expense	______	______	______	______

The MixMax Company
Comparative Balance Sheets
August 1, 19X1 and August 31, 19X1

Assets	8/1/X1	8/31/X1
Cash	$ 41,000	$?
Accounts Receivable	67,000	85,000
Allowance for Doubtful Accounts	(7,280)	(7,600)
Inventory	28,000	44,000
Property, Plant and Equipment	27,000	27,000
Accumulated Depreciation	(2,835)	(3,240)
Total Assets	$ 152,885	$?

Liabilities and Owners' Equities		
Accounts Payable Merchandise	$ 19,000	$ 21,000
Accounts Payable Services	4,260	8,176
Interest Payable	416	815
Taxes Payable	4,802	8,804
Current Portion of Debt	2,984	2,399
Deferred Taxes	396	594
Long-Term Debt	38,627	38,627
Bonds Payable	0	?
Unamortized Bond Discount	0	(3,530)
Common Stock	13,000	13,000
Retained Earnings	69,400	75,700
Total Liabilities and Owners' Equities	$ 152,885	$?

The MixMax Company
August 19X1
T-Accounts

Alternative
to the Income Summary:
Individual Income Accounts

Income Summary

Retained Earnings

Common Stock

Cash

CfO

Financing

Investing

Indirect Method
of Calculating
Cash from Operations

NI

CfO

Allowance for Doubtful Accounts

Accounts Receivable

Inventory

Accumulated Depreciation

Property, Plant and Equipment

The MixMax Company
August 19X1
T-Accounts

Current Portion of Debt

Accounts Payable Merchandise

Accounts Payable Services

Interest Payable

Unamortized Bond Discount

Bonds Payable

Long-Term Debt

Taxes Payable

Deferred Taxes

The MixMax Company
Reconciliation of Income Events to Operating Cash Flow Events
August 19X1

	Income Events	Events not associated with Operating Cash Flows	(Debit) Credit Change in Current Operating Account(s)	**Operating Cash Flow Events**
Sales Revenue				
less: **Bad Debt Expense**				
Net Sales Revenue				
Sales Revenue not associated with Cash Flows from Operations				
Decrease (Increase) in Accounts Receivable				
Increase (Decrease) in Allowance for Doubtful Accounts				
Collections from Customers				
Cost of Goods Sold				
Cost of Goods Sold not associated with Cash Flows from Operations				
Decrease (Increase) in Inventory				
Increase (Decrease) in Accounts Payable Merchandise				
Payments to Suppliers of Merchandise				
Operating Expenses				
Operating Expenses not associated with Cash Flows from Operations				
Increase (Decrease) in Accounts Payable Services				
Payments to Suppliers of Services				
Interest Expense				
Interest Expense not associated with Cash Flows from Operations				
Increase (Decrease) in Interest Payable				
Interest Payment				
Tax Expense				
Tax Expense not associated with Cash Flows from Operations				
Increase (Decrease) in Taxes Payable				
Tax Payment				
Net Income				
Total Income Events not associated with Cash Flows from Operations				
Decrease (Increase) in Net Current Operating Accounts				
Cash Flows from Operating Events				

The MixMax Company
Income Statement
August 19X1

Revenues

Sales Revenue		$ 84,000
Bad Debt Expense		(3,360)
Net Sales Revenue		$ 80,640
Total Revenues		$ 80,640

Expenses

Cost of Goods Sold	$ 56,000	
Operating Expenses	13,280	
Interest Expense	?	
Tax Expense	4,200	
Total Expenses	$?	(?)
Net Income		$?

Statement of Cash Flows
August 19X1

Cash (Outflows) from Operating Events		$ (16,415)
Cash Inflows (Outflows) from Financing Events		
Repayment of Loan	$ (?)	
Issue of Bonds	45,000	
Total Financing Events	$?	?
Increase in Cash		$?

Required:

a. List all of the events that occurred during August 19X1.

b. Fill in all of the question (?) marks.

Additional Exercises: Independent of the problem above.

Complete the schedules on page 31.

Recall the $45,000 loan that The MixMax Company arranged to finance the purchase of its equipment back on January 1, 19X1. Consider the possibility that the company might have issued a 5-year, semiannual coupon bond in place of the loan when the market rate was 12 percent, compounded semiannually.

Using the tables in Appendix 3, complete the following schedules, assuming that the bonds were issued at

a. Par (12 percent coupon rate)
b. Discount (10 percent coupon rate)
c. Premium (14 percent coupon rate)

	Par	**Discount**	**Premium**
Coupon Rate	________	________	________
Market Rate	________	________	________
Length of Period	________	________	________
Number of Periods	________	________	________
First Period's Payment	________	________	________
First Period's Expense	________	________	________
Total First Year's Payments	________	________	________
Total First Year's Expense	________	________	________
Total Periodic Payments	________	________	________
Final Payment	________	________	________
Total Payments	________	________	________
Present Value of Total Payments	________	________	________
Total Expense	________	________	________

The MixMax Company
Comparative Balance Sheets
September 1, 19X1 and September 30, 19X1

Assets	9/1/X1	9/30/X1
Cash	$ 69,000	$?
Accounts Receivable	85,000	98,000
Allowance for Doubtful Accounts	(7,600)	(8,600)
Inventory	44,000	53,000
Property, Plant and Equipment	27,000	27,000
Accumulated Depreciation	(3,240)	(3,645)
Total Assets	$ 214,160	$?
Liabilities and Owners' Equities		
Accounts Payable Merchandise	$ 21,000	$ 25,000
Accounts Payable Services	8,176	5,199
Interest Payable	815	1,214
Taxes Payable	8,804	0
Current Portion of Debt	2,399	1,808
Deferred Taxes	594	792
Long-Term Debt	38,627	38,627
Bonds Payable	48,575	48,575
Unamortized Bond Discount	(3,530)	(3,485)
Common Stock [see note]	13,000	52,000
Additional Paid-in Capital [see note]	0	10,125
Retained Earnings	75,700	?
Total Liabilities and Owners' Equities	$ 214,160	$?

Note:

In order to finance future expansion, The MixMax Company issued an additional 37,700 shares of its common stock (par $1), when the market price was $1.25.

The MixMax Company
September 19X1
T-Accounts

Alternative to the Income Summary: Individual Income Accounts

Income Summary

↓ Retained Earnings ↑

↓ Dividends Payable ↑

↓ Common Stock ↑

↓ Common Stock – Additional Paid-in Capital ↑

↑ Cash ↓

CfO

Financing

Investing

Indirect Method of Calculating Cash from Operations

NI

CfO

↓ **Allowance for Doubtful Accounts** ↑

↑ **Accounts Receivable** ↓

↑ **Inventory** ↓

↓ Accumulated Depreciation ↑

↑ Property, Plant and Equipment ↓

The MixMax Company
September 19X1
T-Accounts

↓ Current Portion of Debt ↑

↓ **Accounts Payable Merchandise** ↑

↓ **Accounts Payable Services** ↑

↓ **Interest Payable** ↑

↑ Unamortized Bond Discount ↓

↓ Bonds Payable ↑

↓ Long-Term Debt ↑

↓ **Taxes Payable** ↑

↓ Deferred Taxes ↑

The MixMax Company
Reconciliation of Income Events to Operating Cash Flow Events
September 19X1

	Income Events	Events not associated with Operating Cash Flows	(Debit) Credit Change in Current Operating Account(s)	**Operating Cash Flow Events**
Sales Revenue				
less: **Bad Debt Expense**				
Net Sales Revenue				
Sales Revenue not associated with Cash Flows from Operations				
Decrease (Increase) in Accounts Receivable				
Increase (Decrease) in Allowance for Doubtful Accounts				
Collections from Customers				
Cost of Goods Sold				
Cost of Goods Sold not associated with Cash Flows from Operations				
Decrease (Increase) in Inventory				
Increase (Decrease) in Accounts Payable Merchandise				
Payments to Suppliers of Merchandise				
Operating Expenses				
Operating Expenses not associated with Cash Flows from Operations				
Increase (Decrease) in Accounts Payable Services				
Payments to Suppliers of Services				
Interest Expense				
Interest Expense not associated with Cash Flows from Operations				
Increase (Decrease) in Interest Payable				
Interest Payment				
Tax Expense				
Tax Expense not associated with Cash Flows from Operations				
Increase (Decrease) in Taxes Payable				
Tax Payment				
Net Income				
Total Income Events not associated with Cash Flows from Operations				
Decrease (Increase) in Net Current Operating Accounts				
Cash Flows from Operating Events				

The MixMax Company
Income Statement
September 19X1

Revenues		
Sales Revenue		$ 91,000
Bad Debt Expense		(3,640)
Net Sales Revenue		$ 87,360
Total Revenues		$ 87,360
Expenses		
Cost of Goods Sold	$ 63,000	
Operating Expenses	?	
Interest Expense	854	
Tax Expense	5,000	
Total Expenses	$?	(?)
Net Income		$?

Statement of Cash Flows
September 19X1

Cash (Outflows) from Operating Events		$ (20,234)
Cash Inflows (Outflows) from Financing Events		
Repayment of Loan	$ (?)	
Payment of Dividend	(1,300)	
Issue of Common Stock	?	
Total Financing Events	$?	?
Increase in Cash		$?

Required:

a. List all of the events that occurred during September 19X1.

b. Fill in all of the question (?) marks.

The MixMax Company
Comparative Balance Sheets
July 1, 19X1 and September 30, 19X1

Assets	7/1/X1	9/30/X1
Cash	$ 44,000	$?
Accounts Receivable	63,000	98,000
Allowance for Doubtful Accounts	(5,600)	(8,600)
Inventory	14,000	53,000
Property, Plant and Equipment	27,000	27,000
Accumulated Depreciation	(2,430)	(3,645)
Total Assets	$ 139,970	$?
Liabilities and Owners' Equities		
Accounts Payable Merchandise	$ 14,500	$ 25,000
Accounts Payable Services	7,760	5,199
Interest Payable	422	1,214
Current Portion of Debt	3,563	1,808
Deferred Taxes	198	792
Long-Term Debt	38,627	38,627
Bonds Payable	0	48,575
Unamortized Bond Discount	0	(3,485)
Common Stock	13,000	52,000
Additional Paid-in Capital	0	10,125
Retained Earnings	61,900	?
Total Liabilities and Owners' Equities	$ 139,970	$?

The MixMax Company
Third Quarter 19X1
T-Accounts

Alternative
to the Income Summary:
Individual Income Accounts

Income Summary

Retained Earnings

Dividends Payable

Common Stock

Common Stock
Additional Paid-in Capital

Cash

CfO

Financing

Investing

Indirect Method
of Calculating
Cash from Operations

NI

CfO

Allowance for
Doubtful Accounts

Accounts Receivable

Inventory

Accumulated Depreciation

Property,
Plant and Equipment

The MixMax Company
Third Quarter 19X1
T-Accounts

Current Portion of Debt

Accounts Payable
Merchandise

Accounts Payable
Services

Interest Payable

Unamortized
Bond Discount

Bonds Payable

Long-Term Debt

Taxes Payable

Deferred Taxes

The MixMax Company
Reconciliation of Income Events to Operating Cash Flow Events
Third Quarter 19X1

	Income Events	Events not associated with Operating Cash Flows	(Debit) Credit Change in Current Operating Account(s)	**Operating Cash Flow Events**
Sales Revenue				
less: **Bad Debt Expense**				
Net Sales Revenue				
Sales Revenue not associated with Cash Flows from Operations				
Decrease (Increase) in Accounts Receivable				
Increase (Decrease) in Allowance for Doubtful Accounts				
Collections from Customers				
Cost of Goods Sold				
Cost of Goods Sold not associated with Cash Flows from Operations				
Decrease (Increase) in Inventory				
Increase (Decrease) in Accounts Payable Merchandise				
Payments to Suppliers of Merchandise				
Operating Expenses				
Operating Expenses not associated with Cash Flows from Operations				
Increase (Decrease) in Accounts Payable Services				
Payments to Suppliers of Services				
Interest Expense				
Interest Expense not associated with Cash Flows from Operations				
Increase (Decrease) in Interest Payable				
Interest Payment				
Tax Expense				
Tax Expense not associated with Cash Flows from Operations				
Increase (Decrease) in Taxes Payable				
Tax Payment				
Net Income				
Total Income Events not associated with Cash Flows from Operations				
Decrease (Increase) in Net Current Operating Accounts				
Cash Flows from Operating Events				

The MixMax Company
Income Statement
Third Quarter 19X1

Revenues		
Sales Revenue		$?
Bad Debt Expense		(9,880)
Net Sales Revenue		$?
Total Revenues		$?
Expenses		
Cost of Goods Sold	$ 161,000	
Operating Expenses	38,490	
Interest Expense	2,130	
Tax Expense	14,200	
Total Expenses	$ 215,820	(215,820)
Net Income		$?

Statement of Cash Flows
Third Quarter 19X1

Cash (Outflows) from Operating Events		$ (39,070)
Cash Inflows (Outflows) from Financing Events		
Repayment of Loan	$ (?)	
Payment of Dividend	(1,300)	
Issue of Bonds	45,000	
Issue of Common Stock	?	
Total Financing Events	$ 89,070	?
Increase in Cash		$?

Required:

a. List all of the events that occurred during the third quarter of 19X1.

b. Fill in all of the question (?) marks.

The MixMax Company
Comparative Balance Sheets
October 1, 19X1 and October 31, 19X1

Assets	10/1/X1	10/31/X1
Cash	$ 94,000	$ 78,000
Marketable Equity Securities [see note]	0	26,000
Accounts Receivable	98,000	131,000
Allowance for Doubtful Accounts	(8,600)	(9,800)
Inventory	53,000	21,000
Property, Plant and Equipment	27,000	?
Accumulated Depreciation	(3,645)	(4,050)
Leasehold Asset	0	44,325
Total Assets	$ 259,755	$?

Liabilities and Owners' Equities		
Accounts Payable Merchandise	$ 25,000	$ 20,000
Accounts Payable Services	5,199	5,878
Interest Payable	1,214	1,953
Taxes Payable	0	9,072
Current Portion of Debt	1,808	1,211
Deferred Taxes	792	1,320
Long-Term Debt	38,627	38,627
Bonds Payable	48,575	48,575
Unamortized Bond Discount	(3,485)	(3,440)
Leasehold Liability	0	33,854
Common Stock	52,000	52,000
Additional Paid-in Capital	10,125	10,125
Retained Earnings	79,900	?
Total Liabilities and Owners' Equities	$ 259,755	$?

Note:

During the month of October 19X1, The MixMax Company purchased Marketable Equity Securities, for cash, as follows:

Security	Purchase Date	Cost	Market Value (as of 10/31/X1)
Alpha	10/1/X1	$ 5,500	$ 5,200
Beta	10/2/X1	9,000	10,000
Gamma	10/9/X1	11,500	11,100
Total		$ 26,000	$ 26,300

The MixMax Company
October 19X1
T-Accounts

Alternative to the Income Summary: Individual Income Accounts

Income Summary

Retained Earnings

Common Stock

Common Stock Additional Paid-in Capital

Cash

CfO

Financing

Investing

Indirect Method of Calculating Cash from Operations

NI

CfO

Allowance for Doubtful Accounts

Accounts Receivable

Inventory

Accumulated Depreciation

Property, Plant and Equipment

Current Marketable Equity Securities

The MixMax Company
October 19X1
T-Accounts

Current Portion of Debt

Accounts Payable Merchandise

Accounts Payable Services

Leasehold Asset

Interest Payable

Unamortized Bond Discount

Bonds Payable

Leasehold Liability

Long-Term Debt

Taxes Payable

Deferred Taxes

The MixMax Company
Reconciliation of Income Events to Operating Cash Flow Events
October 19X1

	Income Events	Events not associated with Operating Cash Flows	(Debit) Credit Change in Current Operating Account(s)	Operating Cash Flow Events
Sales Revenue				
less: **Bad Debt Expense**				
Net Sales Revenue				
Sales Revenue not associated with Cash Flows from Operations				
Decrease (Increase) in Accounts Receivable				
Increase (Decrease) in Allowance for Doubtful Accounts				
Collections from Customers				
Cost of Goods Sold				
Cost of Goods Sold not associated with Cash Flows from Operations				
Decrease (Increase) in Inventory				
Increase (Decrease) in Accounts Payable Merchandise				
Payments to Suppliers of Merchandise				
Operating Expenses				
Operating Expenses not associated with Cash Flows from Operations				
Increase (Decrease) in Accounts Payable Services				
Payments to Suppliers of Services				
Interest Expense				
Interest Expense not associated with Cash Flows from Operations				
Increase (Decrease) in Interest Payable				
Interest Payment				
Tax Expense				
Tax Expense not associated with Cash Flows from Operations				
Increase (Decrease) in Taxes Payable				
Tax Payment				
Net Income				
Total Income Events not associated with Cash Flows from Operations				
Decrease (Increase) in Net Current Operating Accounts				
Cash Flows from Operating Events				

The MixMax Company
Income Statement
October 19X1

Revenues		
Sales Revenue		$ 130,000
Bad Debt Expense		(5,200)
Net Sales Revenue		$ 124,800
Total Revenues		$ 124,800
Expenses		
Cost of Goods Sold	$ 86,000	
Operating Expenses	?	
Interest Expense	1,188	
Tax Expense	9,600	
Total Expenses	$?	(?)
Net Income		$?

Statement of Cash Flows
October 19X1

Cash Inflows from Operating Events		$?
Cash (Outflows) from Financing Events		
Repayment of Loan	$ (597)	
Lease Payment	(?)	
Total Financing Events	$?	(?)
Cash (Outflows) from Investing Events		
Acquisition of Marketable Securities	$ (?)	
Total Investing Events	$ (?)	(?)
(Decrease) in Cash		$ (?)

Schedule of Significant Noncash Financing **and** Investing Events
October 19X1

Inception of Capital Lease	$ 45,000

Required:

a. List all of the events that occurred during October 19X1.

b. Fill in all of the question (?) marks.

Additional Exercises: Independent of the problem above.

Complete the schedules on page 38 and answer the questions on page 39.

a. Recall that The MixMax Company purchased the following equipment on January 1, 19X1:

Unit	Cost	Salvage Value
Truck	$ 18,000	$ 1,800
Wagon	14,400	1,440
Auto	12,600	1,260
	$ 45,000	$ 4,500

with a useful life of 5 years. The company amortizes its long-lived assets on a straight-line basis for financial reporting purposes.

Consider the possibility that the company leased rather than purchased the equipment, and that the lease required five annual payments, at an annual interest rate of 12 percent, with an option to pay either

i. $11,146 each January 1, 19X1 through 19X5 (payments in advance), or
ii. $12,483 each December 31, 19X1 through 19X5 (payments in arrears)

Using the tables in Appendix 3, complete the following schedules for both options, assuming that the lease could be accounted for as either

i. an operating lease, or
ii. a capital lease

	Payment in Advance		Payment in Arrears	
	Operating	**Capital**	**Operating**	**Capital**
Interest Rate	______	______	______	______
Length of Period	______	______	______	______
Number of Periods	______	______	______	______
First Period's Payment	______	______	______	______
First Period's Expense	______	______	______	______
Total First Year's Payments	______	______	______	______
Total First Year's Expense	______	______	______	______
Total Periodic Payments	______	______	______	______
Present Value of Total Payments	______	______	______	______
Total Expense	______	______	______	______

b. *If* the company opted to amortize its leasehold asset using the double-declining balance method for tax purposes and the straight-line method for financial reporting purposes, what effect(s), if any, would it have had on its October financial statements? (Assume a 40 percent tax rate.)

c. *If* the company were required to treat the lease as an operating lease for tax purposes and as a capital lease for financial reporting purposes, what effect(s), if any, would it have had on its October financial statements? (Assume a 40 percent tax rate.)

The MixMax Company
Comparative Balance Sheets
November 1, 19X1 and November 30, 19X1

Assets	11/1/X1	11/30/X1
Cash	$ 78,000	$?
Marketable Equity Securities [see note]	26,000	33,500
Valuation Allowance [see note]	0	(400)
Accounts Receivable	131,000	131,000
Allowance for Doubtful Accounts	(9,800)	(12,300)
Inventory	21,000	?
Property, Plant and Equipment	27,000	27,000
Accumulated Depreciation	(4,050)	(4,455)
Leasehold Asset	44,325	43,650
Total Assets	$ 313,475	$?

Liabilities and Owners' Equities		
Accounts Payable Merchandise	$ 20,000	$ 13,000
Accounts Payable Services	5,878	8,218
Interest Payable	1,953	2,690
Taxes Payable	9,072	17,344
Current Portion of Debt	1,211	609
Deferred Taxes	1,320	1,848
Long-Term Debt	38,627	?
Bonds Payable	48,575	?
Unamortized Bond Discount	(3,440)	(3,395)
Leasehold Liability	33,854	?
Common Stock	52,000	52,000
Additional Paid-in Capital	10,125	10,125
Retained Earnings	94,300	107,500
Total Liabilities and Owners' Equities	$ 313,475	$ 330,995

Note:

The MixMax Company sold all of its shares in Beta for $10,700. The rest of their portfolio was as follows:

Security	Purchase Date	Cost	Market Value (as of 11/30/X1)
Alpha	10/1/X1	$ 5,500	$ 5,600
Gamma	10/9/X1	11,500	11,200
Delta	11/8/X1	16,500	16,300

The MixMax Company
November 19X1
T-Accounts

Alternative to the Income Summary: Individual Income Accounts

Income Summary

Retained Earnings

Common Stock

Common Stock Additional Paid-in Capital

Cash

CfO

Financing

Investing

Indirect Method of Calculating Cash from Operations

NI

CfO

The MixMax Company
November 19X1
T-Accounts

Allowance for Doubtful Accounts

Accounts Receivable

Inventory

Accumulated Depreciation

Property, Plant and Equipment

Valuation Allowance

Current Marketable Equity Securities

Current Portion of Debt

Accounts Payable Merchandise

Accounts Payable Services

Leasehold Asset

Interest Payable

Unamortized Bond Discount

Bonds Payable

Leasehold Liability

Long-Term Debt

Taxes Payable

Deferred Taxes

The MixMax Company
Reconciliation of Income Events to Operating Cash Flow Events
November 19X1

	Income Events	Events not associated with Operating Cash Flows	(Debit) Credit Change in Current Operating Account(s)	**Operating Cash Flow Events**
Sales Revenue				
less: **Bad Debt Expense**				
Net Sales Revenue				
Sales Revenue not associated with Cash Flows from Operations				
Decrease (Increase) in Accounts Receivable				
Increase (Decrease) in Allowance for Doubtful Accounts				
Collections from Customers				
Realized Gain on Sale of Marketable Securities				
Realized Gain not associated with Cash Flows from Operations				
No Current Operating Accounts affected				
Operating Cash Flows associated with the Sale				
Cost of Goods Sold				
Cost of Goods Sold not associated with Cash Flows from Operations				
Decrease (Increase) in Inventory				
Increase (Decrease) in Accounts Payable Merchandise				
Payments to Suppliers of Merchandise				
Operating Expenses				
Operating Expenses not associated with Cash Flows from Operations				
Increase (Decrease) in Accounts Payable Services				
Payments to Suppliers of Services				
Interest Expense				
Interest Expense not associated with Cash Flows from Operations				
Increase (Decrease) in Interest Payable				
Interest Payment				
Net Unrealized Loss in Marketable Securities				
Net Unrealized Loss not associated with Cash Flows from Operations				
No Current Operating Accounts affected				
Operating Cash Flows associated with the Loss				
Tax Expense				
Tax Expense not associated with Cash Flows from Operations				
Increase (Decrease) in Taxes Payable				
Tax Payment				
Net Income				
Total Income Events not associated with Cash Flows from Operations				
Decrease (Increase) in Net Current Operating Accounts				
Cash Flows from Operating Events				

The MixMax Company
Income Statement
November 19X1

Revenues and Gains		
Sales Revenue		$?
Bad Debt Expense		(4,320)
Net Sales Revenue		$?
Realized Gain on Sale of Marketable Securities		?
Total Revenues and Gains		$?
Expenses and Losses		
Cost of Goods Sold	$ 69,000	
Operating Expenses	12,799	
Interest Expense	1,181	
Net Unrealized Loss in Marketable Securities	?	
Tax Expense	8,800	
Total Expenses and Losses	$?	(?)
Net Income		$?

Statement of Cash Flows
November 19X1

Cash Inflows from Operating Events		$?
Cash (Outflows) from Financing Events		
Repayment of Loan	$ (602)	
Total Financing Events	$ (602)	(602)
Cash Inflows (Outflows) from Investing Events		
Acquisition of Marketable Securities	$ (?)	
Sale of Marketable Securities	?	
Total Investing Events	$ (?)	(?)
Increase in Cash		$ 27,000

Required:

a. List all of the events that occurred during November 19X1.

b. Fill in all of the question (?) marks.

The MixMax Company
Comparative Balance Sheets
December 1, 19X1 and December 31, 19X1

Assets	12/1/X1	12/31/X1
Cash	$ 105,000	$ 8,400
Marketable Equity Securities	33,500	0
Valuation Allowance	(400)	?
Accounts Receivable	131,000	106,000
Allowance for Doubtful Accounts	(12,300)	(13,300)
Inventory	8,000	15,000
Investment in Affiliated Companies	0	95,000
Property, Plant and Equipment [see note]	27,000	100,000
Accumulated Depreciation [see note]	(4,455)	(500)
Leasehold Asset	43,650	42,975
Total Assets	$ 330,995	$?

Liabilities and Owners' Equities		
Accounts Payable Merchandise	$ 13,000	$ 10,000
Accounts Payable Services	8,218	13,221
Interest Payable	2,690	3,917
Taxes Payable	17,344	0
Current Portion of Debt	609	14,881
Deferred Taxes	1,848	1,645
Long-Term Debt	38,627	30,830
Bonds Payable	48,575	90,490
Unamortized Bond Discount	(3,395)	(3,350)
Unamortized Bond Premium	0	3,046
Leasehold Liability	33,854	26,770
Common Stock	52,000	52,000
Additional Paid-in Capital	10,125	10,125
Retained Earnings	107,500	?
Total Liabilities and Owners' Equities	$ 330,995	$?

Note:

On December 1, 19X1, The MixMax Company sold all of its property, plant and equipment, leasing new equipment in their place.

The MixMax Company
December 19X1
T-Accounts

Alternative to the Income Summary: Individual Income Accounts

Income Summary

↓ Retained Earnings ↑

↓ Dividends Payable ↑

↓ Common Stock ↑

↓ Common Stock Additional Paid-in Capital ↑

↑ Cash ↓

CfO

Financing

Investing

Indirect Method of Calculating Cash from Operations

NI

CfO

The MixMax Company
December 19X1
T-Accounts

↓ **Allowance for Doubtful Accounts** ↑

↑ **Accounts Receivable** ↓

↑ **Inventory** ↓

↓ Accumulated Depreciation ↑

↑ Property, Plant and Equipment ↓

↓ Valuation Allowance ↑

↑ Current Marketable Equity Securities ↓

↓ Current Portion of Debt ↑

↓ **Accounts Payable Merchandise** ↑

↓ **Accounts Payable Services** ↑

↑ Leasehold Asset ↓

↑ **Dividends Receivable** ↓

↑ Investment in Affiliated Company ↓

↓ **Interest Payable** ↑

↑ Unamortized Bond Discount ↓

↓ Unamortized Bond Premium ↑

↓ Bonds Payable ↑

↓ Leasehold Liability ↑

↓ Long-Term Debt ↑

↓ **Taxes Payable** ↑

↓ Deferred Taxes ↑

The MixMax Company
Reconciliation of Income Events to Operating Cash Flow Events
December 19X1

	Income Events	Events not associated with Operating Cash Flows	(Debit) Credit Change in Current Operating Account(s)	**Operating Cash Flow Events**
Sales Revenue				
less: **Bad Debt Expense**				
Net Sales Revenue				
Sales Revenue not associated with Cash Flows from Operations				
Decrease (Increase) in Accounts Receivable				
Increase (Decrease) in Allowance for Doubtful Accounts				
Collections from Customers				
Net Unrealized Gain in Marketable Securities				
Net Unrealized Gain not associated with Cash Flows from Operations				
No Current Operating Accounts affected				
No Operating Cash Flows associated with the Gain				
Earnings of Affiliated Company				
Earnings not associated with Cash Flows from Operations				
plus: Investments in Affiliated Company				
Decrease (Increase) in Investment in Affiliated Company				
Decrease (Increase) in Dividends Receivable				
Collection of Dividend				
Cost of Goods Sold				
Cost of Goods Sold not associated with Cash Flows from Operations				
Decrease (Increase) in Inventory				
Increase (Decrease) in Accounts Payable Merchandise				
Payments to Suppliers of Merchandise				
Operating Expenses				
Operating Expenses not associated with Cash Flows from Operations				
Increase (Decrease) in Accounts Payable Services				
Payments to Suppliers of Services				
Interest Expense				
Interest Expense not associated with Cash Flows from Operations				
Increase (Decrease) in Interest Payable				
Interest Payment				
Realized Loss on Sale of Marketable Securities				
Realized Loss not associated with Cash Flows from Operations				
No Current Operating Accounts affected				
Operating Cash Flows associated with the Sale				
Tax Expense				
Tax Expense not associated with Cash Flows from Operations				
Increase (Decrease) in Taxes Payable				
Tax Payment				
Net Income				
Total Income Events not associated with Cash Flows from Operations				
Decrease (Increase) in Net Current Operating Accounts				
Cash Flows from Operating Events				

The MixMax Company
Income Statement
December 19X1

Revenues and Gains

Sales Revenue		$?
Bad Debt Expense		(3,520)
Net Sales Revenue		$?
Net Unrealized Gain in Marketable Securities		400
Earnings of Affiliated Companies		8,000
Total Revenues and Gains		$?

Expenses and Losses

Cost of Goods Sold	$ 56,000	
Operating Expenses	20,055	
Interest Expense	1,625	
Realized Loss on Sale of Marketable Securities	1,700	
Tax Expense	5,400	
Total Expenses and Losses	$ 84,780	(84,780)
Net Income		$?

Statement of Cash Flows
December 19X1

Cash Inflows from Operating Events		$ 9,264
Cash Inflows (Outflows) from Financing Events		
Repayment of Loan	$ (?)	
Payment of Dividend	(?)	
Issue of Bonds	45,000	
Total Financing Events	$ 28,791	28,791
Cash Inflows (Outflows) from Investing Events		
Sale of Property, Plant and Equipment	$?	
Acquisition of Property, Plant and Equipment	(?)	
Sale of Marketable Securities	9,800	
Investment in Affiliated Companies	(?)	
Total Investing Events	$?	(?)
(Decrease) in Cash		$ (?)

Required:

a. List all of the events that occurred during December 19X1.

b. Fill in all of the question (?) marks.

The MixMax Company
Comparative Balance Sheets
January 1, 19X1 and December 31, 19X1

Assets	1/1/X1	12/31/X1
Cash	$ 8,400	$ 8,400
Accounts Receivable	1,600	106,000
Allowance for Doubtful Accounts	0	(13,300)
Inventory	7,000	15,000
Prepaid Rent	3,000	0
Investment in Affiliated Companies	0	95,000
Property, Plant and Equipment	0	100,000
Accumulated Depreciation	0	(500)
Leasehold Asset	0	42,975
Total Assets	$ 20,000	$ 353,575

Liabilities and Owners' Equities		
Advances from Customers	$ 1,400	$ 0
Accounts Payable Merchandise	3,600	10,000
Accounts Payable Services	200	13,221
Interest Payable	0	3,917
Current Portion of Debt	0	14,881
Deferred Taxes	0	1,645
Long-Term Debt	0	30,830
Bonds Payable	0	90,490
Unamortized Bond Discount	0	(3,350)
Unamortized Bond Premium	0	3,046
Leasehold Liability	0	26,770
Common Stock	13,000	52,000
Additional Paid-in Capital	0	10,125
Retained Earnings	1,800	100,000
Total Liabilities and Owners' Equities	$ 20,000	$ 353,575

The MixMax Company
19X1
T-Accounts

Alternative to the Income Summary: Individual Income Accounts

Income Summary

↓ Retained Earnings ↑

↓ Dividends Payable ↑

↓ Common Stock ↑

↓ Common Stock — Additional Paid-in Capital ↑

↑ Cash ↓

CfO

Financing

Investing

Indirect Method of Calculating Cash from Operations

NI

CfO

The MixMax Company
19X1
T-Accounts

↓ **Allowance for Doubtful Accounts** ↑

↑ **Accounts Receivable** ↓

↑ **Inventory** ↓

↑ **Prepaid Rent** ↓

↓ Accumulated Depreciation ↑

↑ Property, Plant and Equipment ↓

↓ Current Portion of Debt ↑

↓ **Advances from Customers** ↑

↓ **Accounts Payable Merchandise** ↑

↓ **Accounts Payable Services** ↑

↑ Leasehold Asset ↓

↑ **Dividends Receivable** ↓

↑ Investment in Affiliated Company ↓

↓ **Interest Payable** ↑

↑ Unamortized Bond Discount ↓

↓ Unamortized Bond Premium ↑

↓ Bonds Payable ↑

↓ Leasehold Liability ↑

↓ Long-Term Debt ↑

↓ **Taxes Payable** ↑

↓ Deferred Taxes ↑

The MixMax Company
Reconciliation of Income Events to Operating Cash Flow Events
19X1

	Income Events	Events not associated with Operating Cash Flows	(Debit) Credit Change in Current Operating Account(s)	**Operating Cash Flow Events**
Sales Revenue				
less: **Bad Debt Expense**				
Net Sales Revenue				
Sales Revenue not associated with Cash Flows from Operations				
Decrease (Increase) in Accounts Receivable				
Increase (Decrease) in Advances from Customers				
Increase (Decrease) in Allowance for Doubtful Accounts				
Collections from Customers				
Earnings of Affiliated Company				
Earnings not associated with Cash Flows from Operations				
plus: Investments in Affiliated Company				
Decrease (Increase) in Investment in Affiliated Company				
Decrease (Increase) in Dividends Receivable				
Collection of Dividend				
Cost of Goods Sold				
Cost of Goods Sold not associated with Cash Flows from Operations				
Decrease (Increase) in Inventory				
Increase (Decrease) in Accounts Payable Merchandise				
Payments to Suppliers of Merchandise				
Operating Expenses				
Operating Expenses not associated with Cash Flows from Operations				
Decrease (Increase) in Prepaid Rent				
Increase (Decrease) in Accounts Payable Services				
Payments to Suppliers of Services				
Interest Expense				
Interest Expense not associated with Cash Flows from Operations				
Increase (Decrease) in Interest Payable				
Interest Payment				
Loss on Sale of Property, Plant and Equipment				
Loss on Sale not associated with Cash Flows from Operations				
No Current Operating Accounts affected				
Operating Cash Flows associated with the Sale				
Tax Expense				
Tax Expense not associated with Cash Flows from Operations				
Increase (Decrease) in Taxes Payable				
Tax Payment				
Net Income				
Total Income Events not associated with Cash Flows from Operations				
Decrease (Increase) in Net Current Operating Accounts				
Cash Flows from Operating Events				

The MixMax Company
Income Statement
19X1

Revenues

Sales Revenue		$ 900,000
Bad Debt Expense		(30,000)
Net Sales Revenue		$ 870,000
Earnings of Affiliated Companies		8,000
Total Revenues		$ 878,000

Expenses and Losses

Cost of Goods Sold	$ 525,000	
Operating Expenses	144,379	
Interest Expense	8,741	
Loss on Sale of Property, Plant and Equipment	380	
Tax Expense	79,800	
Total Expenses and Losses	$ 758,300	(758,300)
Net Income		$ 119,700

Statement of Cash Flows
19X1

Cash Inflows from Operating Events		$ 50,349

Cash Inflows (Outflows) from Financing Events

Repayment of Loan	$ (6,373)	
Payment of Dividend	(19,500)	
Issue of Bonds	90,000	
Issue of Common Stock	47,125	
Lease Payment	(11,146)	
Total Financing Events	$ 100,106	100,106

Cash Inflows (Outflows) from Investing Events

Acquisition of Property, Plant and Equipment	$(100,000)	
Sale of Property, Plant and Equipment	38,545	
Acquisition of Marketable Securities	(42,500)	
Sale of Marketable Securities	20,500	
Investment in Affiliated Companies	(67,000)	
Total Investing Events	$(150,455)	(150,455)
Change in Cash		$ 0

Schedule of Significant Noncash Financing and Investing Events
19X1

Acquisition of Property, Plant and Equipment with Debt	$ 45,000
Inception of Capital Lease	45,000

Required:

List all of the events that occurred during 19X1.

Introduction

In this appendix, we will demonstrate the technique of solving a problem similar to the January 19X1 MixMax problem. The objective of this kind of problem is to determine the events that occurred during the period of time covered by a set of financial statements.

The Problem

From the following comparative balance sheets and related statement of cash receipts and disbursements of a merchandising concern

a. Determine the events that occurred during December 19X0

b. Prepare an income statement for the month of December 19X0

Comparative Balance Sheets
December 1, 19X0 and December 31, 19X0

Assets	12/1/X0	12/31/X0
Cash	$ 7,500	$ 8,400
Accounts Receivable	0	1,600
Inventory	5,000	7,000
Prepaid Rent	3,500	3,000
Total Assets	$ 16,000	$ 20,000
Liabilities and Owners' Equities		
Advances from Customers	$ 2,000	$ 1,400
Accounts Payable Merchandise	1,000	3,600
Accounts Payable Services	0	200
Common Stock	13,000	13,000
Retained Earnings	0	1,800
Total Liabilities and Owners' Equities	$ 16,000	$ 20,000

Statement of Cash Receipts and Disbursements
December 19X0

Cash Receipts	
Collections from Credit Customers	$ 5,700
Cash Sales	2,600
Advances from Customers	1,500
Total Cash Receipts	$ 9,800
Cash Disbursements	
Payments to Suppliers of Merchandise	$ 5,400
Payments to Suppliers of Services	2,300
Payment of Taxes	1,200
Total Cash Disbursements	$ 8,900
Excess Cash Receipts over Cash Disbursements	$ 900

How Accounts Work

There are four elements to an account: the beginning balance, events increasing the account, events decreasing the account, and the ending balance. The ending balance of an account is determined by adding the increases in the account to, and subtracting the decreases in the account from, the beginning balance. For example

	Beginning Balance	$	5,000
+	Increases		8,000
-	Decreases		6,000
=	Ending Balance	$	7,000

Since the balance in the account above increased, the total amount of the events increasing the account must have been greater than the total amount of the events decreasing the account. Rearranging the elements from the example above, it is clear that the difference between the beginning balance ($5,000) and ending balance ($7,000) equals the difference between the events increasing ($8,000) and the events decreasing ($6,000) the account.

Therefore, the difference between the beginning balance and the ending balance of an account (<u>magnitude of change</u>) equals the difference between the total amount of the events that increased and decreased the account, and indicates whether the increases were greater or less than the decreases (<u>direction of change</u>).

By comparing the beginning and ending balances (comparative balances) in the accounts, we know the **magnitude** and **direction** of the difference between the events that have increased and decreased an account. For example

	Beginning Balance	$	5,000
+	Increases		?
-	Decreases		?
=	Ending Balance	$	7,000

Since the balance in this account increased by $2,000, you might conclude that **only one** event (in the amount of $2,000) occurred to increase the account:

	Beginning Balance	$	5,000
+	Increases		2,000
-	Decreases		0
=	Ending Balance	$	7,000

But there is an infinite number of combined increases and decreases that could explain the $2,000 increase in the account. For example

		Beginning Balance	$	5,000
	+	Increases		4,000
	-	Decreases		2,000
	=	Ending Balance	$	7,000
or		Beginning Balance	$	5,000
	+	Increases		99,999
	-	Decreases		97,999
	=	Ending Balance	$	7,000

However, if any three of the four elements of an account are known, then the fourth can always be determined. For example

		Beginning Balance	$	5,000
	+	Increases		8,000
	-	Decreases		6,000
	=	Ending Balance	$	?
or		Beginning Balance	$	5,000
	+	Increases		8,000
	-	Decreases		?
	=	Ending Balance	$	7,000
or		Beginning Balance	$	5,000
	+	Increases		?
	-	Decreases		6,000
	=	Ending Balance	$	7,000
or		Beginning Balance	$	?
	+	Increases		8,000
	-	Decreases		6,000
	=	Ending Balance	$	7,000

The T-Account

The T-account is a visual presentation of the relationship between the four elements of an account. For asset accounts, the beginning balance, the increases, and the ending balance are on the debit (Dr.) side and the decreases are on the credit (Cr.) side. For equity accounts (liabilities and owners' equities), the beginning balance, the increases, and the ending balance are on the credit (Cr.) side and the decreases are on the debit (Dr.) side.

↑ Assets	↓	↓ Equities	↑
Beg Bal			Beg Bal
Increases	Decreases	Decreases	Increases
End Bal			End Bal

The Effects of Events on Balance Sheet Accounts

Cash

Cash Receipts increase the account, and
Cash Disbursements decrease the account.

Accounts Receivable

Credit Sales Revenues increase the account, and
Collections from Credit Customers decrease the account.

Inventory

Purchases of Inventory increases the account, and
Cost of Goods Sold decreases the account.

Prepaid Rent

Prepayment of Rent increases the account, and
Utilization of Rented Space (Rent Expense) decreases the account.

Advances from Customers

Advances from Customers increase the account, and
Sales Revenues Previously Paid For decrease the account.

Accounts Payable Merchandise

Credit Purchases of Inventory increase the account, and
Payments to Suppliers of Merchandise decrease the account.

Accounts Payable Services

Utilization of Services on Credit increases the account, and
Payments to Suppliers of Services decrease the account.

Common Stock

Issue of Common Stock increases the account, and
Repurchase of Common Stock decreases the account.

Retained Earnings

Net Income increases the account, and the
Declaration of Dividends decreases the account.

The T-accounts on pages 52 and 53 incorporate the discussion on the previous pages. For each account listed in the comparative balance sheets on page 47, a corresponding T-account is drawn indicating

a. The side on which the balances of an account [(BB) and (EB)] appear, (BB) representing the beginning balance and (EB) the ending balance
b. The side on which an account increases (↑) and decreases (↓)
c. The events that increase and decrease an account

```
↑                                                                        ↓
----------------------------------Cash-----------------------------------
                                    |
BB                                  |
                                    |
                                    |
                          Receipts  |  Disbursements
                                    |
                                    |
EB                                  |
                                    |

↑                                                                        ↓
-------------------------Accounts Receivable-----------------------------
                                    |
BB                                  |
                                    |
                            Credit  |  Collections
                             Sales  |  from Credit
                          Revenues  |  Customers
                                    |
EB                                  |
                                    |

↑                                                                        ↓
-------------------------------Inventory---------------------------------
                                    |
BB                                  |
                                    |
                         Purchases  |  Cost
                                of  |  of Goods
                         Inventory  |  Sold
                                    |
EB                                  |
                                    |

↑                                                                        ↓
-----------------------------Prepaid Rent--------------------------------
                                    |
BB                                  |
                                    |
                        Prepayment  |  Rent Expense
                                of  | (Utilization of
                              Rent  |  Rented Space)
                                    |
EB                                  |
                                    |
```

↓ **Advances from Customers** ↑

	BB
Sales Revenues Previously Paid For	Advances from Customers
	EB

↓ **Accounts Payable Merchandise** ↑

	BB
Payments to Suppliers of Merchandise	Credit Purchases of Inventory
	EB

↓ **Accounts Payable Services** ↑

	BB
Payments to Suppliers of Services	Operating Expenses (Utilization of Services on Credit)
	EB

↓ **Common Stock** ↑

	BB
Repurchase of Common Stock	Issue of Common Stock
	EB

↓ **Retained Earnings** ↑

	BB
Declaration of Dividends	Net Income
	EB

Explanation of the Changes in the Balance Sheet Accounts

From the comparative balance sheets (page 47), we can determine the magnitude and direction of the changes in the accounts. From the effects of events on balance sheet accounts (pages 50 and 51), we can determine the relationship between the events that increased and decreased each account, and which event was greater.

Cash

The balance in the Cash account increased by $900.

Since Cash Receipts increase the account and Cash Disbursements decrease the account, Cash Receipts must have been greater than Cash Disbursements by $900 (the difference of the balances).

Accounts Receivable

The balance in the Accounts Receivable account increased by $1,600.

Since Credit Sales Revenues increase the account and Collections from Credit Customers decrease the account, Credit Sales Revenues must have been greater than Collections from Credit Customers by $1,600 (the difference of the balances).

Inventory

The balance in the Inventory account increased by $2,000.

Since Purchases of Inventory increases the account and Cost of Goods Sold decreases the account, Purchases of Inventory must have been greater than Cost of Goods Sold by $2,000 (the difference of the balances).

Prepaid Rent

The balance in the Prepaid Rent account decreased by $500.

Since Prepaying Rent increases the account and Utilization of Rented Space (Rent Expense) decreases the account, Rent Expense must have been greater than Prepayment of Rent by $500 (the difference of the balances).

↑ Cash ↓

BB	7,500		
		Receipts	Disbursements
EB	8,400		

↑ Accounts Receivable ↓

BB	0		
		Credit Sales Revenues	Collections from Credit Customers
EB	1,600		

↑ Inventory ↓

BB	5,000		
		Purchases of Inventory	Cost of Goods Sold
EB	7,000		

↑ Prepaid Rent ↓

BB	3,500		
		Prepayment of Rent	Rent Expense (Utilization of Rented Space)
EB	3,000		

Advances from Customers

The balance in the Advances from Customers account decreased by $600. Since Advances from Customers increase the account and Sales Revenues (from customers who paid in advance) decrease the account, Sales Revenues Previously Paid For must have been greater than Advances from Customers by $600 (the difference of the balances).

Accounts Payable Merchandise

The balance in the Accounts Payable Merchandise increased by $2,600. Since Credit Purchases of Inventory increase the account and Payments to Suppliers of Merchandise decrease the account, Credit Purchases of Inventory must have been greater than Payments to Suppliers of Merchandise by $2,600 (the difference of the balances).

Accounts Payable Services

The balance in the Accounts Payable Services account increased by $200. Since Utilization of Services on Credit increase the account and Payments to Suppliers of Services decrease the account, Utilization of Services on Credit (Operating Expenses) must have been greater than Payments to Suppliers of Services by $200 (the difference of the balances).

Common Stock

The balance in the Common Stock account did not change.
Since Issue of Common Stock increases the account and Repurchase of Common Stock decreases the account, Issue of Common Stock must have been equal to Repurchase of Common Stock (no change in Common Stock).

Retained Earnings

The balance in the Retained Earnings account increased by $1,800.
Since Net Income increases the account and the Declaration of Dividends decreases the account, Net Income must have been greater than the Declaration of Dividends by $1,800 (the difference of the balances).

Advances from Customers

↓	↑		
		2,000	BB
Sales Revenues Previously Paid For	Advances from Customers		
		1,400	EB

Accounts Payable Merchandise

↓	↑		
		1,000	BB
Payments to Suppliers of Merchandise	Credit Purchases of Inventory		
		3,600	EB

Accounts Payable Services

↓	↑		
		0	BB
Payments to Suppliers of Services	Operating Expenses (Utilization of Services on Credit)		
		200	EB

Common Stock

↓	↑		
		13,000	BB
Repurchase of Common Stock	Issue of Common Stock		
		13,000	EB

Retained Earnings

↓	↑		
		0	BB
Declaration of Dividends	Net Income		
		1,800	EB

Having set up T-accounts indicating the events that increase and decrease each account, their beginning balances (BB), and their ending balances (EB), we are ready to record the given events.

Recording the Given Events

From the statement of cash receipts and disbursements, we know that certain events occurred. Journal entries for events (1) through (3) are straightforward. The entries are

		Dr.	Cr.
(1)	Collections from Credit Customers		
	Dr. Cash	5,700	
	Cr. Accounts Receivable		5,700
(2)	Cash Sales		
	Dr. Cash	2,600	
	Cr. Sales Revenues (I/S)[2]		2,600
(3)	Advances from Customers		
	Dr. Cash	1,500	
	Cr. Advances from Customers		1,500

However, for events (4) through (6) we must make an assumption. The assumption is that when we make a payment, it will always reduce a liability. Therefore the entries for the remaining given events are

		Dr.	Cr.
(4)	Payments to Suppliers of Merchandise		
	Dr. Accounts Payable Merchandise	5,400	
	Cr. Cash		5,400
(5)	Payments to Suppliers of Services		
	Dr. Accounts Payable Services	2,300	
	Cr. Cash		2,300
(6)	Payment of Taxes		
	Dr. Taxes Payable	1,200	
	Cr. Cash		1,200

The next step is to record the entries for the given events in the T-accounts. Recording events (1) through (5) is straightforward, but recording event (6) poses a problem.

Payment of Taxes has the effect of reducing Taxes Payable (Dr.) and Cash (Cr.). Recall that we set up T-accounts for those accounts that appeared in the comparative balance sheets (page 47). Since Taxes Payable was not listed, no T-account was set up.

Thought Question

Can there be events, reported in either the income statement or the statement of cash receipts and disbursements, that affect accounts that are not listed in the balance sheet?

---

[2]Events marked with (I/S) are revenues and expenses. Though revenues and expenses increase and decrease Retained Earnings, respectively, they are not recorded directly in Retained Earnings. Instead, they are recorded in **temporary accounts** from which an income statement is generated, and then **closed** to Retained Earnings.

The absence of an account in the comparative balance sheets **does not** imply that there were no events that affected the account during the period. It only means that the beginning **and** ending balances of the account were $0, and that the events that increased the account were equal in amount to the events that decreased the account.

Since Taxes Payable was not listed in the comparative balance sheets, its beginning and ending balances were $0. Open a new T-account for Taxes Payable indicating a beginning balance ($0), the event that increases it (Tax Expense), the event that decreases it (Payment of Taxes), and an ending balance ($0). Now record its effect as you would any other event:

(6) Payment of Taxes		
Dr. Taxes Payable	1,200	
Cr. Cash		1,200

Taxes Payable

↓				
			0	BB
(6) 1,200	Payment of Taxes (Given)	Tax Expense		
			0	EB

↑ (increases on right side)

We have now recorded all of the **given** events in this problem in the T-accounts on pages 60 and 61. If after recording the given events, the differences between the beginning balances (BB) and the ending balances (EB) of all of the accounts have not been explained (the differences in the balances do not equal the differences between the events affecting the accounts), then additional events must have occurred during the period. These additional events must be **derived.**

↑ Cash ↓

BB	7,500				
(1)	5,700	Receipts	Disbursements	5,400	(4)
(2)	2,600	(Given)	(Given)	2,300	(5)
(3)	1,500			1,200	(6)
EB	8,400				

↑ Accounts Receivable ↓

BB	0				
		Credit Sales Revenues (To Be Derived)	Collections from Credit Customers (Given)	5,700	(1)
EB	1,600				

↑ Inventory ↓

BB	5,000		
		Purchases of Inventory (To Be Derived)	Cost of Goods Sold (To Be Derived)
EB	7,000		

↑ Prepaid Rent ↓

BB	3,500		
		Prepayment of Rent (To Be Derived)	Rent Expense (Utilization of Rented Space) (To Be Derived)
EB	3,000		

Advances from Customers

		Debit ↓	Credit ↑		
				2,000	BB
		Sales Revenues Previously Paid For (To Be Derived)	Advances from Customers (Given)	1,500	(3)
				1,400	EB

Accounts Payable Merchandise

		Debit ↓	Credit ↑		
				1,000	BB
(4)	5,400	Payments to Suppliers of Merchandise (Given)	Credit Purchases of Inventory (To Be Derived)		
				3,600	EB

Accounts Payable Services

		Debit ↓	Credit ↑		
				0	BB
(5)	2,300	Payments to Suppliers of Services (Given)	Operating Expenses (Utilization of Services on Credit) (To Be Derived)		
				200	EB

Taxes Payable

		Debit ↓	Credit ↑		
				0	BB
(6)	1,200	Payment of Taxes (Given)	Tax Expense (To Be Derived)		
				0	EB

Common Stock

		Debit ↓	Credit ↑		
				13,000	BB
		Repurchase of Common Stock (To Be Derived)	Issue of Common Stock (To Be Derived)		
				13,000	EB

Retained Earnings

		Debit ↓	Credit ↑		
				0	BB
		Declaration of Dividends (To Be Derived)	Net Income (To Be Derived)		
				1,800	EB

Deriving Events

To derive the remaining events that occurred during the month, we can begin with any one of the following accounts: Accounts Receivable, Accounts Payable Services, Accounts Payable Merchandise, Advances from Customers, and Taxes Payable.

Thought Question

Why couldn't we (or shouldn't we) begin with Cash, Inventory, Prepaid Rent, Common Stock, or Retained Earnings?

Let's begin with Accounts Payable Merchandise. Recall the previous discussion of the changes in this account (page 56). Since Accounts Payable Merchandise increased by $2,600, Credit Purchases of Inventory must have been greater than Payments to Suppliers of Merchandise by $2,600. Since Payments to Suppliers of Merchandise were $5,400, then Credit Purchases of Inventory must have been $8,000 ($5,400 + $2,600).

The journal entry to record this event is

(A) Credit Purchases of Inventory

	Dr.	Cr.
Dr. Inventory	8,000	
Cr. Accounts Payable Merchandise		8,000

and the effects of recording this event in the two accounts are

↓ Accounts Payable Merchandise ↑

				1,000	BB
(4) 5,400	Payments to Suppliers of Merchandise		Credit Purchases of Inventory	8,000	(A)
				3,600	EB

↑ Inventory ↓

BB	5,000				
(A)	8,000	Purchases of Inventory	Cost of Goods Sold	6,000	(B)
EB	7,000				

Authors' Convention

Notice that the event Payments to Suppliers of Merchandise is referenced by (4), and that the event Credit Purchases of Inventory is referenced by the letter (A). **Given events** have numerical references and **derived events** have alphabetic references.

If we continue this process, we can derive the following events:

		Dr.	Cr.
(B)	Cost of Goods Sold		
	Dr. Cost of Goods Sold (I/S)	6,000	
	Cr. Inventory		6,000
(C)	Operating Expenses		
	Dr. Operating Expenses (I/S)	2,500	
	Cr. Accounts Payable Services		2,500
(D)	Tax Expense		
	Dr. Tax Expense (I/S)	1,200	
	Cr. Taxes Payable		1,200
(E)	Sales Revenues		
	Dr. Advances from Customers	2,100	
	Cr. Sales Revenues (I/S)		2,100
(F)	Sales Revenues		
	Dr. Accounts Receivable	7,300	
	Cr. Sales Revenues (I/S)		7,300

Now the only unreconciled accounts are Prepaid Rent, Common Stock, and Retained Earnings. From the statement of cash receipts and disbursements (the complete listing of all cash events), we can see that there were no Prepayments of Rent. Since the account decreased by $500, and the debit (Dr.) to Prepaid Rent was $0, Rent Expense must have been $500. The journal entry to record this is

		Dr.	Cr.
(G)	Rent Expense		
	Dr. Rent Expense (I/S)	500	
	Cr. Prepaid Rent		500

Similarly, we can see that there was neither a cash receipt from the Issue of Common Stock nor a cash disbursement for the Repurchase of Common Stock. Therefore, both the debit (Dr.) and credit (Cr.) effects (for the issue and repurchase of common stock, respectively) to Common Stock were $0.

Finally, by closing all of the revenue and expense events to Retained Earnings

		Dr.	Cr.
(H)	Closing Net Income to Retained Earnings		
	Dr. Sales Revenues	12,000	
	Cr. Cost of Goods Sold		6,000
	Cr. Operating Expenses		2,500
	Cr. Tax Expense		1,200
	Cr. Rent Expense		500
	Cr. Retained Earnings		1,800

we have explained the $1,800 increase in the Retained Earnings account. From this we can conclude that no dividends were declared.

==

Thought Question

How else could we have concluded that dividends were not declared?

==

The last step in solving a problem of this type is to record the effects of all of the **derived** events in the T-accounts. After recording the derived events, all of the differences in the balances in all of the accounts have been unambiguously explained by all of the events -- given and derived -- that occurred.

Cash

↑						↓
BB		7,500				
	(1)	5,700	Receipts	Disbursements	5,400	(4)
	(2)	2,600			2,300	(5)
	(3)	1,500			1,200	(6)
EB		8,400				

Accounts Receivable

↑						↓
BB		0				
	(F)	7,300	Credit Sales Revenues	Collections from Credit Customers	5,700	(1)
EB		1,600				

Inventory

↑						↓
BB		5,000				
	(A)	8,000	Purchases of Inventory	Cost of Goods Sold	6,000	(B)
EB		7,000				

Prepaid Rent

↑						↓
BB		3,500				
		0	Prepayment of Rent	Rent Expense (Utilization of Rented Space)	500	(G)
EB		3,000				

↓ Advances from Customers ↑

				2,000	BB
(E)	2,100	Sales Revenues Previously Paid For	Advances from Customers	1,500	(3)
				1,400	EB

↓ Accounts Payable Merchandise ↑

				1,000	BB
(4)	5,400	Payments to Suppliers of Merchandise	Credit Purchases of Inventory	8,000	(A)
				3,600	EB

↓ Accounts Payable Services ↑

				0	BB
(5)	2,300	Payments to Suppliers of Services	Operating Expenses (Utilization of Services on Credit)	2,500	(C)
				200	EB

↓ Taxes Payable ↑

				0	BB
(6)	1,200	Payment of Taxes	Tax Expense	1,200	(D)
				0	EB

↓ Common Stock ↑

				13,000	BB
	0	Repurchase of Common Stock	Issue of Common Stock	0	
				13,000	EB

↓ Retained Earnings ↑

				0	BB
	0	Declaration of Dividends	Net Income	1,800	(H)
				1,800	EB

The T-accounts below are temporary accounts. They represent the revenue and expense events that occurred during the month, and are **closed** to Retained Earnings [see event (H), page 63].

Sales Revenues

(H) 12,000	Closing Entry	Sales Revenues	2,600	(2)
		Sales Revenues	2,100	(E)
		Sales Revenues	7,300	(F)

Cost of Goods Sold

(B) 6,000	Cost of Goods Sold	Closing Entry	6,000	(H)

Operating Expenses

(C) 2,500	Operating Expenses (Utilization of Services on Credit)	Closing Entry	2,500	(H)

Tax Expense

(D) 1,200	Tax Expense	Closing Entry	1,200	(H)

Rent Expense

(G) 500	Rent Expense (Utilization of Rented Space)	Closing Entry	500	(H)

The income statement that follows is a result of the closing process -- a summary of the revenues and expenses.

Income Statement
December 19X0

Revenues

Sales Revenues		$ 12,000
Total Revenues		$ 12,000

Expenses

Cost of Goods Sold	$ 6,000	
Operating Expenses	2,500	
Rent Expense	500	
Tax Expense	1,200	
Total Expenses	$ 10,200	(10,200)
Net Income		$ 1,800

The Double T-Account

The events approach[3] to accounting stresses the determination of accounting events from financial statements.

==

Thought Question

In determining events, do you need to know the amount of the beginning and ending balances, or just their difference?

==

In order to derive events, we only need to know the difference between the beginning and ending balances of the balance sheet accounts. The double T-account nets the beginning and ending balances of the T-account. The net changes in the ten T-accounts on pages 64 and 65, are explained below, and the T-accounts are presented on pages 69 and 70.

Cash

Since the beginning balance of Cash was $7,500 and the ending balance $8,400, Cash increased during the month by $900.
This is a **Debit Change** of $900.

Accounts Receivable

Since the beginning balance of Accounts Receivable was $0 and the ending balance $1,600, Accounts Receivable increased during the month by $1,600.
This is a **Debit Change** of $1,600.

Inventory

Since the beginning balance of Inventory was $5,000 and the ending balance $7,000, Inventory increased during the month by $2,000.
This is a **Debit Change** of $2,000.

Prepaid Rent

Since the beginning balance of Prepaid Rent was $3,500 and the ending balance $3,000, Prepaid Rent decreased during the month by $500.
This is a **Credit Change** of $500.

---

[3] George H. Sorter, Monroe J. Ingberman, and Hillel M. Maximon, *Financial Accounting: An Events and Cash Flow Approach*, McGraw-Hill, New York, 1990.

Advances from Customers

Since the beginning balance of Advances from Customers was $2,000 and the ending balance $1,400, Advances from Customers decreased during the month by $600. This is a **Debit Change** of $600.

Accounts Payable Merchandise

Since the beginning balance of Accounts Payable Merchandise was $1,000 and the ending balance $3,600, Accounts Payable Merchandise increased during the month by $2,600. This is a **Credit Change** of $2,600.

Accounts Payable Services

Since the beginning balance of Accounts Payable Services was $0 and the ending balance was $200, Accounts Payable Services increased during the month by $200. This is a **Credit Change** of $200.

Taxes Payable

Since the beginning balance of Taxes Payable was $0 and the ending balance $0, Taxes Payable did not change during the month.
The **No Change** is represented by an equal sign crossing the vertical bar.

Common Stock

Since the beginning balance of Common Stock was $13,000 and the ending balance $13,000, Common Stock did not change during the month.
The **No Change** is represented by an equal sign crossing the vertical bar.

Retained Earnings

Since the beginning balance of Retained Earnings was $0 and the ending balance $1,800, Retained Earnings increased during the month by $1,800. This is a **Credit Change** of $1,800.

The double T-accounts presented below combine the discussion on the two previous pages with the results in the single T-accounts that appear on pages 64 and 65.

The entries that appear below the second horizontal line in the double T-account are identical to the entries that appear below the horizontal line in the single T-accounts on pages 64 and 65. The only difference between the two presentations is that both the beginning and ending balances appear in the single T-account, but just their difference appears in the double T-account.

Cash

↑					↓
	900				
(1)	5,700	Receipts	Disbursements	5,400	(4)
(2)	2,600			2,300	(5)
(3)	1,500			1,200	(6)

Accounts Receivable

↑					↓
	1,600				
(F)	7,300	Sales Revenues	Collections from Credit Customers	5,700	(1)

Inventory

↑					↓
	2,000				
(A)	8,000	Purchases of Inventory	Cost of Goods Sold	6,000	(B)

Prepaid Rent

↑					↓
				500	
	0	Prepayment of Rent	Rent Expense (Utilization of Rented Space)	500	(G)

↓ **Advances from Customers** ↑

	600				
(E)	2,100	Sales Revenues Previously Paid For	Advances from Customers	1,500	(3)

↓ **Accounts Payable Merchandise** ↑

				2,600	
(4)	5,400	Payments to Suppliers of Merchandise	Credit Purchases of Inventory	8,000	(A)

↓ **Accounts Payable Services** ↑

				200	
(5)	2,300	Payments to Suppliers of Services	Operating Expenses (Utilization of Services on Credit)	2,500	(C)

↓ **Taxes Payable** ↑

=

(6)	1,200	Payment of Taxes	Tax Expense	1,200	(D)

↓ **Common Stock** ↑

=

	0	Repurchase of Common Stock	Issue of Common Stock	0	

↓ **Retained Earnings** ↑

				1,800	
	0	Declaration of Dividends	Net Income	1,800	(H)

Concluding Remarks

Refer to events (6) and (D) on pages 58 and 63, respectively.

(6)	Payment of Taxes		
	Dr. Taxes Payable	1,200	
	Cr. Cash		1,200

(D)	Tax Expense		
	Dr. Tax Expense (I/S)	1,200	
	Cr. Taxes Payable		1,200

It is obvious that the debit (Dr.) effect of event (6) offsets the credit (Cr.) effect of event (D) and that the net effect of the two events is

Dr. Tax Expense (I/S)	1,200	
Cr. Cash		1,200

Why, then, did we record events (6) and (D), rather than just the "net effect" of the two events? The accrual method of accounting distinguishes between **expenses** and **expenditures** because expenses and their related expenditures generally occur at different points in time and are often quantified at different dollar amounts. Therefore, accountants record (and report) expenses and expenditures as two separate and distinct events.

Authors' Conventions

Unless explicitly determinable:

Expenses will **never** be paid for in cash. Expenses will either decrease an existing asset or increase a payable. Similarly, revenues will **never** be received in cash. Revenues will either increase a receivable or decrease an existing liability.

Cash disbursements will **always** decrease a liability, and cash receipts will **always** decrease a receivable.

Finally, notice that we have solved the December 19X0 problem anew. The cash events [(3), (5), (7), (9), parts of (1) and (6) and the comparative balance sheets from the December 19X0 problem] were presented in this problem, and we were required to prepare an income statement [events (1), (2), (8), (10), and part of (6) from the December 19X0 problem].

Alternatively, we could have prepared a statement of cash receipts and disbursements if an income statement had been presented with the comparative balance sheets.

Introduction

In this section, we show the relationship between accounting events, the accounts they affect, and the resultant financial statements: comparative balance sheets, income statement, and statement of cash flows.

Contents of this Appendix

Each of the following accounting events is represented by a journal entry, and is referenced by a three-digit number. The referencing is in terms of income (revenues and gains, expenses and losses), cash (receipts and disbursements), or events other than income or cash. The effects of each event can be traced through the accompanying T-accounts, and the results can be seen in the accompanying financial statements.

Legend

Revenues	(101 - 102)	
Gain	(111 -)	
Expenses	(201 - 205)	
Loss	(211 -)	
Closing Net Income	(- 399)	
Cash Receipts	(401 - 402)	Operating Events
	(421 - 422)	Debt Financing Events
	(431 -)	Equity Financing Event
	(441 - 443)	Investing Events
Cash Disbursements	(501 - 504)	Operating Events
	(521 -)	Debt Financing Event
	(531 - 532)	Equity Financing Events
	(541 - 543)	Investing Events
Neither Income nor Cash	(601 - 602)	Operating Events
	(631 - 632)	Equity Financing Events
	(641 -)	Investing Event
	(651 -)	Financing **and** Investing Event
	(661 - 664)	Neither Operating, **nor** Financing **nor** Investing Events

How to Use this Appendix

Suppose you were given comparative balance sheets and a statement of cash receipts and disbursements, and were required to determine Cost of Goods Sold for the period. All you would have to know is that Cost of Goods Sold is an expense, and from the list of journal entries for expenses, you would find journal entry (202)

Cost of Goods Sold
    Dr. Cost of Goods Sold (I/S)
        Cr. Inventory

Thus, the account that needs to be examined is Inventory. By tracing the effect of the event to the Inventory account, you would see that the credit (Cr.) entry to the Inventory account is for the Cost of Goods Sold, and the debit (Dr.) entry is for the Credit Purchases of Inventory (602). Tracing journal entry (602)

Credit Purchases of Inventory
    Dr. Inventory
        Cr. Accounts Payable Merchandise

to Accounts Payable Merchandise reveals that the credit (Cr.) entry to the account is for the Credit Purchases of Inventory, and the debit (Dr.) entry is for Payments to Suppliers of Merchandise (501). Since the event Payments to Suppliers of Merchandise is reported in the statement of cash receipts and disbursements, Cost of Goods can easily be determined.

↓ Accounts Payable Merchandise	↑	↑ Inventory	↓
	BB	BB	
Payments to Suppliers of Merchandise	Credit Purchases of Inventory	Purchases of Inventory	Cost of Goods Sold
Given →→→	**Derived** →→→→→→→→→→→→→→→→→	**Derived** →→→	**Derived**
	EB	EB	

Beginning with Payments to Suppliers of Merchandise [the debit (Dr.) entry to Accounts Payable Merchandise], and the beginning and ending balances in Accounts Payable Merchandise (as provided in the comparative balance sheets), you can derive Credit Purchases of Inventory [the credit (Cr.) entry to Accounts Payable Merchandise]. From Credit Purchases of Inventory [the debit (Dr.) entry to Inventory], and the beginning and ending balances in the Inventory account, you can derive Cost of Goods Sold [the credit (Cr.) entry to Inventory].

Conversely, if comparative balance sheets and an income statement were presented, you would be required to derive Payments to Suppliers of Merchandise having been given Cost of Goods Sold.

↓ Accounts Payable Merchandise	↑	↑ Inventory	↓
	BB	BB	
Payments to Suppliers of Merchandise	Credit Purchases of Inventory	Purchases of Inventory	Cost of Goods Sold
Derived ←←←	**Derived** ←←←←←←←←←←←←←←←←←	**Derived** ←←←	**Given**
	EB	EB	

Journal Entries for Revenues

(101) Sales Revenue
Dr. Accounts Receivable
Dr. Advances from Customers
Cr. Sales Revenue (I/S)

(102) Earnings of Affiliated Company
Dr. Investment in Affiliated Company
Cr. Earnings of Affiliated Company (I/S)

Journal Entry for Gain

(111) Reversal of Previous Decline in Value of
Current Marketable Securities
Dr. Valuation Allowance
Cr. Net Unrealized Gain in
Current Marketable Securities (I/S)

Journal Entries for Expenses *

(201) Bad Debt Expense (Contra-Revenue)
Dr. Bad Debt Expense (I/S)
Cr. Allowance for Doubtful Accounts

(202) Cost of Goods Sold
Dr. Cost of Goods Sold (I/S)
Cr. Inventory

(203) Operating Expenses
Dr. Operating Expenses (I/S)
Cr. Prepaid Rent
Cr. Accounts Payable Services
Cr. Accumulated Depreciation
Cr. Leasehold Asset

(204) Interest Expense
Dr. Interest Expense (I/S)
Cr. Interest Payable

(204) Interest Expense
Dr. Interest Expense (I/S)
Cr. Interest Payable
Cr. Unamortized Bond Discount

(204) Interest Expense
Dr. Unamortized Bond Premium
Dr. Interest Expense (I/S)
Cr. Interest Payable

(205) Tax Expense
Dr. Tax Expense (I/S)
Cr. Taxes Payable

(205) Tax Expense
Dr. Tax Expense (I/S)
Cr. Taxes Payable
Cr. Deferred Taxes

(205) Tax Expense
Dr. Deferred Taxes
Dr. Tax Expense (I/S)
Cr. Taxes Payable

Journal Entry for Loss

(211) Decline in Market Value of
Current Marketable Securities
Dr. Net Unrealized Loss in
Current Marketable Securities (I/S)
Cr. Valuation Allowance

Journal Entry to Close Net Income to Retained Earnings

(399) Closing Net Income to Retained Earnings
Dr. Income Summary
Cr. Retained Earnings

* Rent Expense and Depreciation Expense are included in Operating Expenses (203).

Journal Entries for Cash Receipts

(401) Collections from Customers
Dr. Cash
Cr. Accounts Receivable
Cr. Advances from Customers

(402) Collection of Cash Dividends
Dr. Cash
Cr. Dividends Receivable

(421) Borrowing from the Bank (long-term)
Dr. Cash
Cr. Long-Term Debt

(422) Issue of Bonds (at par)
Dr. Cash
Cr. Bonds Payable

(422) Issue of Bonds (at discount)
Dr. Unamortized Bond Discount
Dr. Cash
Cr. Bonds Payable

(422) Issue of Bonds (at premium)
Dr. Cash
Cr. Bonds Payable
Cr. Unamortized Bond Premium

(431) Issue of Common Stock (at par)
Dr. Cash
Cr. Common Stock

(431) Issue of Common Stock (in excess of par)
Dr. Cash
Cr. Common Stock
Cr. Additional Paid-in Capital

(441) Sale of Property, Plant and Equipment
Dr. Cash
Dr. Accumulated Depreciation
Cr. Property, Plant and Equipment

(441) Sale of Property, Plant and Equipment (at a loss)
Dr. Loss on Sale of PPE (I/S)
Dr. Cash
Dr. Accumulated Depreciation
Cr. Property, Plant and Equipment

(441) Sale of Property, Plant and Equipment (for a gain)
Dr. Cash
Dr. Accumulated Depreciation
Cr. Property, Plant and Equipment
Cr. Gain on Sale of PPE (I/S)

(442) Sale of Marketable Securities
Dr. Cash
Cr. Marketable Securities

(442) Sale of Marketable Securities (at a loss)
Dr. Realized Loss on Sale of Securities (I/S)
Dr. Cash
Cr. Marketable Securities

(442) Sale of Marketable Securities (for a gain)
Dr. Cash
Cr. Marketable Securities
Cr. Realized Gain on Sale of Securities (I/S)

(443) Sale of Investment in Affiliated Company
Dr. Cash
Cr. Investment in Affiliated Company

Journal Entries for Cash Disbursements

(501) Payments to Suppliers of Merchandise
Dr. Accounts Payable Merchandise
Cr. Cash

(502) Payments to Suppliers of Services
Dr. Prepaid Rent
Dr. Accounts Payable Services
Cr. Cash

(503) Payment of Interest
Dr. Interest Payable
Cr. Cash

(504) Payment of Taxes
Dr. Taxes Payable
Cr. Cash

(521) Repayment of Debt
Dr. Current Portion of Debt
Cr. Cash

(531) Repurchase of Common Stock (at par)
Dr. Common Stock
Cr. Cash

(531) Repurchase of Common Stock (in excess of par)
Dr. Additional Paid-in Capital
Dr. Common Stock
Cr. Cash

(532) Payment of Cash Dividends
Dr. Dividends Payable
Cr. Cash

(541) Purchase of Property, Plant and Equipment
Dr. Property, Plant and Equipment
Cr. Cash

(541) Acquisition of Property, Plant and Equipment
Dr. Property, Plant and Equipment
Cr. Long-Term Debt

(542) Purchase of Marketable Securities
Dr. Marketable Securities
Cr. Cash

(543) Investment in Affiliated Company
Dr. Investment in Affiliated Company
Cr. Cash

Events affecting <u>neither</u> Cash <u>nor</u> Income

(601) Writeoffs
    Dr. Allowance for Doubtful Accounts
        Cr. Accounts Receivable

(602) Credit Purchase of Inventory
    Dr. Inventory
        Cr. Accounts Payable Merchandise

(631) Declaration of Stock Dividends (at par)
    Dr. Retained Earnings
        Cr. Common Stock

(632) Declaration of Cash Dividends
    Dr. Retained Earnings
        Cr. Dividends Payable

(641) Dividends Declared by Affiliated Company
    Dr. Dividends Receivable
        Cr. Investment in Affiliated Company

(651) Inception of Capital Lease
    Dr. Leasehold Asset
        Cr. Leasehold Liability

(661) Reclassification of Long-Term Debt
    Dr. Long-Term Debt
        Cr. Current Portion of Debt

(662) Reclassification of Bonds
    Dr. Net Bonds Payable
        Cr. Current Portion of Debt

(663) Reclassification of Leasehold Liability
    Dr. Leasehold Liability
        Cr. Current Portion of Debt

(664) Reclassification of Marketable Securities
    Dr. Investment in Affiliated Company
        Cr. Marketable Securities

(631) Declaration of Stock Dividends (in excess of par)
    Dr. Retained Earnings
        Cr. Common Stock
        Cr. Additional Paid-in Capital

(664) Reclassification of Marketable Securities
    Dr. Valuation Allowance
    Dr. Investment in Affiliated Company
        Cr. Marketable Securities

↑ ↓

Cash			
	Cash Receipts from:	Cash Disbursements for:	
(401)	Customers	Suppliers of Merchandise	(501)
(402)	Dividends	Suppliers of Services	(502)
		Interest	(503)
		Taxes	(504)
	Operations		
(421)	Borrowing from the Bank	Repayment of Debt	(521)
(422)	Issue of Bonds		
(431)	Issue of Common Stock	Repurchase of Common Stock	(531)
		Payment of Cash Dividends	(532)
(441)	Sale of Property, Plant and Equipment	Purchase of Property, Plant and Equipment	(541)
(442)	Sale of Marketable Securities	Purchase of Marketable Securities	(542)
(443)	Sale of Affiliated Company	Investment in Affiliated Company	(543)

Income Summary			
(201)	Bad Debt Expense	Sales Revenue	(101)
(202)	Cost of Goods Sold	Earnings of Affiliated Company	(102)
(203)	Operating Expenses		
(204)	Interest Expense		
(205)	Tax Expense		
(211)	Net Unrealized Loss in Current Marketable Securities	Net Unrealized Gain in Current Marketable Securities	(111)
(441)	Loss on Sale of Property, Plant and Equipment	Gain on Sale of Property, Plant and Equipment	(441)
(442)	Loss on Sale of Marketable Securities	Gain on Sale of Marketable Securities	(442)
(399)	Net Income		

Statement of Cash Flows

Cash Flows from Operating Events

(401) Collections from Customers
(402) Collection of Dividends

Total Operating Cash Inflows:

(501) Payments to Suppliers of Merchandise
(502) Payments to Suppliers of Services
(503) Payment of Interest
(504) Payment of Taxes

Total Operating Cash Outflows:

Total Cash Flows from Operating Events:

Cash Flows from Financing Events

(421) Borrowing from the Bank
(521) Repayment of Debt
(422) Issue of Bonds
(431) Issue of Common Stock
(531) Repurchase of Common Stock
(532) Payment of Cash Dividends

Total Cash Flows from Financing Events:

Cash Flows from Investing Events

(441) Sale of Property, Plant and Equipment
(541) Purchase of Property, Plant and Equipment
(442) Sale of Marketable Securities
(542) Purchase of Marketable Securities
(443) Sale of Affiliated Company
(543) Investment in Affiliated Company

Total Cash Flows from Investing Events:

Increase (Decrease) in Cash

Significant Non-Cash Financing and Investing Events

(651) Inception of Capital Lease

Income Statement

Revenues and Gains

(101) Sales Revenue
(201) Less: Bad Debt Expense
Net Sales Revenue
(102) Earnings of Affiliated Company
(111) Net Unrealized Gain in Current Marketable Securities
(441) Gain on Sale of Property, Plant and Equipment
(442) Realized Gain on Sale of Marketable Securities

Total Revenues and Gains:

Expenses and Losses

(202) Cost of Goods Sold
(203) Operating Expenses
(204) Interest Expense
(205) Tax Expense
(211) Net Unrealized Loss in Current Marketable Securities
(441) Loss on Sale of Property, Plant and Equipment
(442) Realized Loss on Sale of Marketable Securities

Total Expenses and Losses:

(399) **Net Income**

Investment in Affiliated Company

↑		↓	
(102)	Earnings of Affiliated Company	Sale of Investment in Affiliated Company	(443)
(543)	Investment in Affiliated Company	Dividends Declared by Affiliated Company	(641)
(664)	Reclassification of Marketable Securities		

Allowance for Doubtful Accounts

↓		↑	
(601)	Writeoffs	Bad Debt Expense	(201)

Dividends Receivable

↑		↓	
(641)	Dividends Declared by Affiliated Company	Collection of Dividends	(402)

Accounts Receivable

↑		↓	
(101)	Credit Sales Revenue	Collections from Credit Customers	(401)
		Writeoffs	(601)

Advances from Customers

↓		↑	
(101)	Deferred Sales Revenue	Advances from Customers	(401)

Inventory

↑		↓	
(602)	Credit Purchase of Inventory	Cost of Goods Sold	(202)

Accounts Payable Merchandise

↓		↑	
(501)	Payments to Suppliers of Merchandise	Credit Purchase of Inventory	(602)

Prepaid Rent

↑		↓	
(502)	Prepayment for Rented Space	Rent Expense (Operating Expense)	(203)

Accounts Payable Services

↓		↑	
(502)	Payments to Suppliers of Services	Operating Expenses	(203)

Property, Plant and Equipment

↑		↓	
(541)	Purchase of Property, Plant and Equipment	Disposal of Property, Plant and Equipment (original cost)	(441)

Accumulated Depreciation

↓		↑	
(441)	Accumulated Depreciation associated with disposed Property, Plant and Equipment	Depreciation Expense (Operating Expense)	(203)

Leasehold Asset

↑		↓	
(651)	Inception of Capital Lease	Amortization of Leasehold Asset (Operating Expense)	(203)

Leasehold Liability

↓		↑	
(663)	Reclassification of Leasehold Liability	Inception of Capital Lease	(651)

Current Marketable Securities

↑		↓	
(542)	Purchase of Marketable Securities	Sale of Marketable Securities	(442)
		Reclassification of Marketable Securities	(664)

Valuation Allowance
Current Marketable Securities

↓		↑	
(111)	Reversal of Previous Decline in Value of Marketable Securities	Decline in Market Value of Marketable Securities	(211)
(664)	Reclassification of Marketable Securities		

Deferred Taxes

↓	↑
(205) Reversal of Deferred Taxes	Deferral of Taxes (205)

Taxes Payable

↓	↑
(504) Payment of Taxes	Currently Payable Tax Expense (205)

Interest Payable

↓	↑
(503) Payment of Interest	Currently Payable Interest Expense (204)

Unamortized Bond Premium

↓	↑
(204) Amortization of Bond Premium	Premium on Issue of Bonds (422)
(662) Reclassification of Bonds Payable	

Unamortized Bond Discount

↑	↓
(422) Discount on Issue of Bonds	Amortization of Bond Discount (204)
	Reclassification of Bonds Payable (662)

Bonds Payable

↓	↑
(662) Reclassification of Bonds Payable	Issue of Bonds (422)

Current Portion of Debt

↓	↑
(521) Repayment of Debt	Reclassification of Long-Term Debt (661)
	Reclassification of Bonds Payable (662)
	Reclassification of Leasehold Liability (663)

Long-Term Debt

↓	↑
(661) Reclassification of Long-Term Debt	Borrowing (421)
	Acquisition of Property, Plant and Equipment (541)

Retained Earnings

↓	↑
(631) Declaration of Stock Dividends	Net Income (399)
(632) Declaration of Cash Dividends	

Dividends Payable

↓	↑
(532) Payment of Cash Dividends	Declaration of Cash Dividends (632)

Common Stock

↓	↑
(531) Repurchase of Common Stock	Issue of Common Stock (431)
	Declaration of Stock Dividends (631)

Additional Paid-in Capital — Common Stock

↓	↑
(531) Repurchase of Common Stock	Issue of Common Stock (431)
	Declaration of Stock Dividends (631)

Balance Sheet

Assets

Cash
Marketable Equity Securities
  Valuation Allowance
Accounts Receivable
  Allowance for Doubtful Accounts
Inventory
Prepaid Rent
Dividends Receivable
Investment in Affiliated Company
Property, Plant and Equipment
  Accumulated Depreciation
Leasehold Asset

Total Assets

Liabilities and Owners' Equities

Advances from Customers
Accounts Payable Merchandise
Accounts Payable Services
Interest Payable
Taxes Payable
Current Portion of Debt
Dividends Payable
Deferred Taxes
Long-Term Debt
Bonds Payable
  Unamortized Bond Discount
Unamortized Bond Premium
Leasehold Liability
Common Stock
Additional Paid-in Capital
Retained Earnings

Total Liabilities and Owners' Equities

Note: Account titles in **bold** are operating accounts.

Present Value of $1.00

n	1/2%	1%	1 1/2%	2%	3%	4 1/2%	5%	6%	7%	9%	10%	12%	15%	18%	n
1	0.995025	0.990099	0.985222	0.980392	0.970874	0.956938	0.952381	0.943396	0.934579	0.917431	0.909091	0.892857	0.869565	0.847458	1
2	0.990075	0.980296	0.970662	0.961169	0.942596	0.915730	0.907029	0.889996	0.873439	0.841680	0.826446	0.797194	0.756144	0.718184	2
3	0.985149	0.970590	0.956317	0.942322	0.915142	0.876297	0.863838	0.839619	0.816298	0.772183	0.751315	0.711780	0.657516	0.608631	3
4	0.980248	0.960980	0.942184	0.923845	0.888487	0.838561	0.822702	0.792094	0.762895	0.708425	0.683013	0.635518	0.571753	0.515789	4
5	0.975371	0.951466	0.928260	0.905731	0.862609	0.802451	0.783526	0.747258	0.712986	0.649931	0.620921	0.567427	0.497177	0.437109	5
6	0.970518	0.942045	0.914542	0.887971	0.837484	0.767896	0.746215	0.704961	0.666342	0.596267	0.564474	0.506631	0.432328	0.370432	6
7	0.965690	0.932718	0.901027	0.870560	0.813092	0.734828	0.710681	0.665057	0.622750	0.547034	0.513158	0.452349	0.375937	0.313925	7
8	0.960885	0.923483	0.887711	0.853490	0.789409	0.703185	0.676839	0.627412	0.582009	0.501866	0.466507	0.403883	0.326902	0.266038	8
9	0.956105	0.914340	0.874592	0.836755	0.766417	0.672904	0.644609	0.591898	0.543934	0.460428	0.424098	0.360610	0.284262	0.225456	9
10	0.951348	0.905287	0.861667	0.820348	0.744094	0.643928	0.613913	0.558395	0.508349	0.422411	0.385543	0.321973	0.247185	0.191064	10
11	0.946615	0.896324	0.848933	0.804263	0.722421	0.616199	0.584679	0.526788	0.475093	0.387533	0.350494	0.287476	0.214943	0.161919	11
12	0.941905	0.887449	0.836387	0.788493	0.701380	0.589664	0.556837	0.496969	0.444012	0.355535	0.318631	0.256675	0.186907	0.137220	12
13	0.937219	0.878663	0.824027	0.773033	0.680951	0.564272	0.530321	0.468839	0.414964	0.326179	0.289664	0.229174	0.162528	0.116288	13
14	0.932556	0.869963	0.811849	0.757875	0.661118	0.539973	0.505068	0.442301	0.387817	0.299246	0.263331	0.204620	0.141329	0.098549	14
15	0.927917	0.861349	0.799852	0.743015	0.641862	0.516720	0.481017	0.417265	0.362446	0.274538	0.239392	0.182696	0.122894	0.083516	15
16	0.923300	0.852821	0.788031	0.728446	0.623167	0.494469	0.458112	0.393646	0.338735	0.251870	0.217629	0.163122	0.106865	0.070776	16
17	0.918707	0.844377	0.776385	0.714163	0.605016	0.473176	0.436297	0.371364	0.316574	0.231073	0.197845	0.145644	0.092926	0.059980	17
18	0.914136	0.836017	0.764912	0.700159	0.587395	0.452800	0.415521	0.350344	0.295864	0.211994	0.179859	0.130040	0.080805	0.050830	18
19	0.909588	0.827740	0.753607	0.686431	0.570286	0.433302	0.395734	0.330513	0.276508	0.194490	0.163508	0.116107	0.070265	0.043077	19
20	0.905063	0.819544	0.742470	0.672971	0.553676	0.414643	0.376889	0.311805	0.258419	0.178431	0.148644	0.103667	0.061100	0.036506	20
22	0.896080	0.803396	0.720688	0.646839	0.521893	0.379701	0.341850	0.277505	0.225713	0.150182	0.122846	0.082643	0.046201	0.026218	22
24	0.887186	0.787566	0.699544	0.621721	0.491934	0.347703	0.310068	0.246979	0.197147	0.126405	0.101526	0.065882	0.034934	0.018829	24
26	0.878380	0.772048	0.679021	0.597579	0.463695	0.318402	0.281241	0.219810	0.172195	0.106393	0.083905	0.052521	0.026415	0.013523	26
28	0.869662	0.756836	0.659099	0.574375	0.437077	0.291571	0.255094	0.195630	0.150402	0.089548	0.069343	0.041869	0.019974	0.009712	28
30	0.861030	0.741923	0.639762	0.552071	0.411987	0.267000	0.231377	0.174110	0.131367	0.075371	0.057309	0.033378	0.015103	0.006975	30
36	0.835645	0.698925	0.585090	0.490223	0.345032	0.205028	0.172657	0.122741	0.087535	0.044941	0.032349	0.016910	0.006529	0.002584	36
42	0.811009	0.658419	0.535089	0.435304	0.288959	0.157440	0.128840	0.086527	0.058329	0.026797	0.018260	0.008567	0.002823	0.000957	42
48	0.787098	0.620260	0.489362	0.386538	0.241999	0.120898	0.096142	0.060998	0.038867	0.015978	0.010307	0.004340	0.001220	0.000355	48
54	0.763893	0.584313	0.447542	0.343234	0.202670	0.092837	0.071743	0.043001	0.025899	0.009527	0.005818	0.002199	0.000528	0.000131	54
60	0.741372	0.550450	0.409296	0.304782	0.169733	0.071289	0.053536	0.030314	0.017257	0.005681	0.003284	0.001114	0.000228	0.000049	60

Future Value of $1.00

n	1/2%	1%	1 1/2%	2%	3%	4 1/2%	5%	6%	7%	9%	10%	12%	15%	18%	n
1	1.005000	1.010000	1.015000	1.020000	1.030000	1.045000	1.050000	1.060000	1.070000	1.090000	1.100000	1.120000	1.150000	1.180000	1
2	1.010025	1.020100	1.030225	1.040400	1.060900	1.092025	1.102500	1.123600	1.144900	1.188100	1.210000	1.254400	1.322500	1.392400	2
3	1.015075	1.030301	1.045678	1.061208	1.092727	1.141166	1.157625	1.191016	1.225043	1.295029	1.331000	1.404928	1.520875	1.643032	3
4	1.020151	1.040604	1.061364	1.082432	1.125509	1.192519	1.215506	1.262477	1.310796	1.411582	1.464100	1.573519	1.749006	1.938778	4
5	1.025251	1.051010	1.077284	1.104081	1.159274	1.246182	1.276282	1.338226	1.402552	1.538624	1.610510	1.762342	2.011357	2.287758	5
6	1.030378	1.061520	1.093443	1.126162	1.194052	1.302260	1.340096	1.418519	1.500730	1.677100	1.771561	1.973823	2.313061	2.699554	6
7	1.035529	1.072135	1.109845	1.148686	1.229874	1.360862	1.407100	1.503630	1.605781	1.828039	1.948717	2.210681	2.660020	3.185474	7
8	1.040707	1.082857	1.126493	1.171659	1.266770	1.422101	1.477455	1.593848	1.718186	1.992563	2.143589	2.475963	3.059023	3.758859	8
9	1.045911	1.093685	1.143390	1.195093	1.304773	1.486095	1.551328	1.689479	1.838459	2.171893	2.357948	2.773079	3.517876	4.435454	9
10	1.051140	1.104622	1.160541	1.218994	1.343916	1.552969	1.628895	1.790848	1.967151	2.367364	2.593742	3.105848	4.045558	5.233836	10
11	1.056396	1.115668	1.177949	1.243374	1.384234	1.622853	1.710339	1.898299	2.104852	2.580426	2.853117	3.478550	4.652391	6.175926	11
12	1.061678	1.126825	1.195618	1.268242	1.425761	1.695881	1,795856	2.012196	2.252192	2.812665	3.138428	3.895976	5.350250	7.287593	12
13	1.066986	1.138093	1.213552	1.293607	1.468534	1.772196	1.885649	2.132928	2.409845	3.065805	3.452271	4.363493	6.152788	8.599359	13
14	1.072321	1.149474	1.231756	1.319479	1.512590	1.851945	1.979932	2.260904	2.578534	3.341727	3.797498	4.887112	7.075706	10.14724	14
15	1.077683	1.160969	1.250232	1.345868	1.557967	1.935282	2.078928	2.396558	2.759032	3.642482	4.177248	5.473566	8.137062	11.97375	15
16	1.083071	1.172579	1.268986	1.372786	1.604706	2.022370	2.182875	2.540352	2.952164	3.970306	4.594973	6.130394	9.357621	14.12902	16
17	1.088487	1.184304	1.288020	1.400241	1.652848	2.113377	2.292018	2.692773	3.158815	4.327633	5.054470	6.866041	10.76126	16.67225	17
18	1.093929	1.196147	1.307341	1.428246	1.702433	2.208479	2.406619	2.854339	3.379932	4.717120	5.559917	7.689966	12.37545	19.67325	18
19	1.099399	1.208109	1.326951	1.456811	1.753506	2.307860	2.526950	3.025600	3.616528	5.141661	6.115909	8.612762	14.23177	23.21444	19
20	1.104896	1.220190	1.346855	1.485947	1.806111	2.411714	2.653298	3.207135	3.869684	5.604411	6.727500	9.646293	16.36654	27.39303	20
22	1.115972	1.244716	1.387564	1.545980	1.916103	2.633652	2.925261	3.603537	4.430402	6.658600	8.140275	12.10031	21.64475	38.14206	22
24	1.127160	1.269735	1.429503	1.608437	2.032794	2.876014	3.225100	4.048935	5.072367	7.911083	9.849733	15.17863	28.62518	53.10901	24
26	1.138460	1.295256	1.472710	1.673418	2.156591	3.140679	3.555673	4.549383	5.807353	9.399158	11.91818	19.04007	37.85680	73.94898	26
28	1.149873	1.321291	1.517222	1.741024	2.287928	3.429700	3.920129	5.111687	6.648838	11.16714	14.42099	23.88387	50.06561	102.9666	28
30	1.161400	1.347849	1.563080	1.811362	2.427262	3.745318	4.321942	5.743491	7.612255	13.26768	17.44940	29.95992	66.21177	143.3706	30
36	1.196681	1.430769	1.709140	2.039887	2.898278	4.877378	5.791816	8.147252	11.42394	22.25123	30.91268	59.13557	153.1519	387.0368	36
42	1.233033	1.518790	1.868847	2.297244	3.460696	6.351615	7.761588	11.55703	17.14426	37.31753	54.76370	116.7231	354.2495	1044.827	42
48	1.270489	1.612226	2.043478	2.587070	4.132252	8.271456	10.40127	16.39387	25.72891	62.58524	97.01723	230.3908	819.4007	2820.567	48
54	1.309083	1.711410	2.234428	2.913461	4.934125	10.77159	13.93870	23.25502	38.61215	104.9617	171.8719	454.7505	1895.324	7614.272	54
60	1.348850	1.816697	2.443220	3.281031	5.891603	14.02741	18.67919	32.98769	57.94643	176.0313	304.4816	897.5969	4383.999	20555.14	60

Present Value of an Annuity of $1.00 in *Arrears*

n	1/2%	1%	1 1/2%	2%	3%	4 1/2%	5%	6%	7%	9%	10%	12%	15%	18%	n
1	0.995025	0.990099	0.985222	0.980392	0.970874	0.956938	0.952381	0.943396	0.934579	0.917431	0.909091	0.892857	0.869565	0.847458	1
2	1.985099	1.970395	1.955883	1.941561	1.913470	1.872668	1.859410	1.833393	1.808018	1.759111	1.735537	1.690051	1.625709	1.565642	2
3	2.970248	2.940985	2.912200	2.883883	2.828611	2.748964	2.723248	2.673012	2.624316	2.531295	2.486852	2.401831	2.283225	2.174273	3
4	3.950496	3.901966	3.854385	3.807729	3.717098	3.587526	3.545951	3.465106	3.387211	3.239720	3.169865	3.037349	2.854978	2.690062	4
5	4.925866	4.853431	4.782645	4.713460	4.579707	4.389977	4.329477	4.212364	4.100197	3.889651	3.790787	3.604776	3.352155	3.127171	5
6	5.896384	5.795476	5.697187	5.601431	5.417191	5.157872	5.075692	4.917324	4.766540	4.485919	4.355261	4.111407	3.784483	3.497603	6
7	6.862074	6.728195	6.598214	6.471991	6.230283	5.892701	5.786373	5.582381	5.389289	5.032953	4.868419	4.563757	4.160420	3.811528	7
8	7.822959	7.651678	7.485925	7.325481	7.019692	6.595886	6.463213	6.209794	5.971299	5.534819	5.334926	4.967640	4.487322	4.077566	8
9	8.779064	8.566018	8.360517	8.162237	7.786109	7.268790	7.107822	6.801692	6.515232	5.995247	5.759024	5.328250	4.771584	4.303022	9
10	9.730412	9.471305	9.222185	8.982585	8.530203	7.912718	7.721735	7.360087	7.023582	6.417658	6.144567	5.650223	5.018769	4.494086	10
11	10.67703	10.36763	10.07112	9.786848	9.252624	8.528917	8.306414	7.886875	7.498674	6.805191	6.495061	5.937699	5.233712	4.656005	11
12	11.61893	11.25508	10.90751	10.57534	9.954004	9.118581	8.863252	8.383844	7.942686	7.160725	6.813692	6.194374	5.420619	4.793225	12
13	12.55615	12.13374	11.73153	11.34837	10.63496	9.682852	9.393573	8.852683	8.357651	7.486904	7.103356	6.423548	5.583147	4.909513	13
14	13.48871	13.00370	12.54338	12.10625	11.29607	10.22283	9.898641	9.294984	8.745468	7.786150	7.366687	6.628168	5.724476	5.008062	14
15	14.41662	13.86505	13.34323	12.84926	11.93794	10.73955	10.37966	9.712249	9.107914	8.060688	7.606080	6.810864	5.847370	5.091578	15
16	15.33993	14.71787	14.13126	13.57771	12.56110	11.23402	10.83777	10.10590	9.446649	8.312558	7.823709	6.973986	5.954235	5.162354	16
17	16.25863	15.56225	14.90765	14.29187	13.16612	11.70719	11.27407	10.47726	9.763223	8.543631	8.021553	7.119630	6.047161	5.222334	17
18	17.17277	16.39827	15.67256	14.99203	13.75351	12.15999	11.68959	10.82760	10.05909	8.755625	8.201412	7.249670	6.127966	5.273164	18
19	18.08236	17.22601	16.42617	15.67846	14.32380	12.59329	12.08532	11.15812	10.33560	8.950115	8.364920	7.365777	6.198231	5.316241	19
20	18.98742	18.04555	17.16864	16.35143	14.87747	13.00794	12.46221	11.46992	10.59401	9.128546	8.513564	7.469444	6.259331	5.352746	20
22	20.78406	19.66038	18.62082	17.65805	15.93692	13.78442	13.16300	12.04158	11.06124	9.442425	8.771540	7.644646	6.358663	5.409901	22
24	22.56287	21.24339	20.03041	18.91393	16.93554	14.49548	13.79864	12.55036	11.46933	9.706612	8.984744	7.784316	6.433771	5.450949	24
26	24.32402	22.79520	21.39863	20.12104	17.87684	15.14661	14.37519	13.00317	11.82578	9.928972	9.160945	7.895660	6.490564	5.480429	26
28	26.06769	24.31644	22.72672	21.28127	18.76411	15.74287	14.89813	13.40616	12.13711	10.11613	9.306567	7.984423	6.533508	5.501601	28
30	27.79405	25.80771	24.01584	22.39646	19.60044	16.28889	15.37245	13.76483	12.40904	10.27365	9.426914	8.055184	6.565980	5.516806	30
36	32.87102	30.10751	27.66068	25.48884	21.83225	17.66604	16.54685	14.62099	13.03521	10.61176	9.676508	8.192414	6.623137	5.541201	36
42	37.79830	34.15811	30.99405	28.23479	23.70136	18.72355	17.42321	15.22454	13.45245	10.81337	9.817397	8.261939	6.647848	5.550238	42
48	42.58032	37.97396	34.04255	30.67312	25.26671	19.53561	18.07716	15.65003	13.73047	10.93358	9.895926	8.297163	6.658531	5.553586	48
54	47.22135	41.56866	36.83054	32.83828	26.57766	20.15918	18.56515	15.94998	13.91573	11.00525	9.941817	8.315008	6.663149	5.554826	54
60	51.72556	44.95504	39.38027	34.76089	27.67556	20.63802	18.92929	16.16143	14.03918	11.04799	9.967157	8.324049	6.665146	5.555285	60

Future Value of an Annuity of $1.00 in *Arrears*

n	1/2%	1%	1 1/2%	2%	3%	4 1/2%	5%	6%	7%	9%	10%	12%	15%	18%	n
1	1.000000	1.000000	1.000000	1.000000	1.000000	1.000000	1.000000	1.000000	1.000000	1.000000	1.000000	1.000000	1.000000	1.000000	1
2	2.005000	2.010000	2.015000	2.020000	2.030000	2.045000	2.050000	2.060000	2.070000	2.090000	2.100000	2.120000	2.150000	2.180000	2
3	3.015025	3.030100	3.045225	3.060400	3.090900	3.137025	3.152500	3.183600	3.214900	3.278100	3.310000	3.374400	3.472500	3.572400	3
4	4.030100	4.060401	4.090903	4.121608	4.183627	4.278191	4.310125	4.374616	4.439943	4.573129	4.641000	4.779328	4.993375	5.215432	4
5	5.050251	5.101005	5.152267	5.204040	5.309136	5.470710	5.525631	5.637093	5.750739	5.984711	6.105100	6.352847	6.742381	7.154210	5
6	6.075502	6.152015	6.229551	6.308121	6.468410	6.716892	6.801913	6.975319	7.153291	7.523335	7.715610	8.115189	8.753738	9.441968	6
7	7.105879	7.213535	7.322994	7.434283	7.662462	8.019152	8.142008	8.393838	8.654021	9.200435	9.487171	10.08901	11.06680	12.14152	7
8	8.141409	8.285671	8.432839	8.582969	8.892336	9.380014	9.549109	9.897468	10.25980	11.02847	11.43589	12.29969	13.72682	15.32700	8
9	9.182116	9.368527	9.559332	9.754628	10.15911	10.80211	11.02656	11.49132	11.97799	13.02104	13.57948	14.77566	16.78584	19.08585	9
10	10.22803	10.46221	10.70272	10.94972	11.46388	12.28821	12.57789	13.18079	13.81645	15.19293	15.93742	17.54874	20.30372	23.52131	10
11	11.27917	11.56683	11.86326	12.16872	12.80780	13.84118	14.20679	14.97164	15.78360	17.56029	18.53117	20.65458	24.34928	28.75514	11
12	12.33556	12.68250	13.04121	13.41209	14.19203	15.46403	15.91713	16.86994	17.88845	20.14072	21.38428	24.13313	29.00167	34.93107	12
13	13.39724	13.80933	14.23683	14.68033	15.61779	17.15991	17.71298	18.88214	20.14064	22.95338	24.52271	28.02911	34.35192	42.21866	13
14	14.46423	14.94742	15.45038	15.97394	17.08632	18.93211	19.59863	21.01507	22.55049	26.01919	27.97498	32.39260	40.50471	50.81802	14
15	15.53655	16.09690	16.68214	17.29342	18.59891	20.78405	21.57856	23.27597	25.12902	29.36092	31.77248	37.27971	47.58041	60.96527	15
16	16.61423	17.25786	17.93237	18.63929	20.15688	22.71934	23.65749	25.67253	27.88805	33.00340	35.94973	42.75328	55.71747	72.93901	16
17	17.69730	18.43044	19.20136	20.01207	21.76159	24.74171	25.84037	28.21288	30.84022	36.97370	40.54470	48.88367	65.07509	87.06804	17
18	18.78579	19.61475	20.48938	21.41231	23.41444	26.85508	28.13238	30.90565	33.99903	41.30134	45.59917	55.74971	75.83636	103.7403	18
19	19.87972	20.81090	21.79672	22.84056	25.11687	29.06356	30.53900	33.75999	37.37896	46.01846	51.15909	63.43968	88.21181	123.4135	19
20	20.97912	22.01900	23.12367	24.29737	26.87037	31.37142	33.06595	36.78559	40.99549	51.16012	57.27500	72.05244	102.4436	146.6280	20
22	23.19443	24.47159	25.83758	27.29898	30.53678	36.30338	38.50521	43.39229	49.00574	62.87334	71.40275	92.50258	137.6316	206.3448	22
24	25.43196	26.97346	28.63352	30.42186	34.42647	41.68920	44.50200	50.81558	58.17667	76.78981	88.49733	118.1552	184.1678	289.4945	24
26	27.59191	29.52563	31.51397	33.67091	38.55304	47.57064	51.11345	59.15638	68.67647	93.32398	109.1818	150.3339	245.7120	405.2721	26
28	29.97452	32.12910	34.48148	37.05121	42.93092	53.99333	58.40258	68.52811	80.69769	112.9682	134.2099	190.6989	327.1041	566.4809	28
30	32.28002	34.78489	37.53868	40.56808	47.57542	61.00707	66.43885	79.05819	94.46079	136.3075	164.4940	241.3327	434.7451	790.9480	30
36	39.33610	43.07688	47.27597	51.99437	63.27594	86.16397	95.83632	119.1209	148.9135	236.1247	299.1268	484.4631	1014.346	2144.649	36
42	46.60654	51.87899	57.92314	64.86222	82.02320	118.9248	135.2318	175.9505	230.6322	403.5281	537.6370	964.3595	2354.997	5799.038	42
48	54.09783	61.22261	69.56522	79.35352	104.4084	161.5879	188.0254	256.5645	353.2701	684.2804	960.1723	1911.590	5456.005	15664.26	48
54	61.81669	71.14105	82.29517	95.67307	131.1375	217.1464	258.7739	370.9170	537.3164	1155.130	1708.719	3781.255	12628.82	42295.96	54
60	69.77003	81.66967	96.21465	114.0515	163.0534	289.4980	353.5837	533.1282	813.5204	1944.792	3034.816	7471.641	29219.99	114189.7	60

Future Value of an Annuity of $1.00 in *Advance*

n	1/2%	1%	1 1/2%	2%	3%	4 1/2%	5%	6%	7%	9%	10%	12%	15%	18%	n
1	1.005000	1.010000	1.015000	1.020000	1.030000	1.045000	1.050000	1.060000	1.070000	1.090000	1.100000	1.120000	1.150000	1.180000	1
2	2.015025	2.030100	2.045225	2.060400	2.090900	2.137025	2.152500	2.183600	2.214900	2.278100	2.310000	2.374400	2.472500	2.572400	2
3	3.030100	3.060401	3.090903	3.121608	3.183627	3.278191	3.310125	3.374616	3.439943	3.573129	3.641000	3.779328	3.993375	4.215432	3
4	4.050251	4.101005	4.152267	4.204040	4.309136	4.470710	4.525631	4.637093	4.750739	4.984711	5.105100	5.352847	5.742381	6.154210	4
5	5.075502	5.152015	5.229551	5.308121	5.468410	5.716892	5.801913	5.975319	6.153291	6.523335	6.715610	7.115189	7.753738	8.441968	5
6	6.105879	6.213535	6.322994	6.434283	6.662462	7.019152	7.142008	7.393838	7.654021	8.200435	8.487171	9.089012	10.06680	11.14152	6
7	7.141409	7.285671	7.432839	7.582969	7.892336	8.380014	8.549109	8.897468	9.259803	10.02847	10.43589	11.29969	12.72682	14.32700	7
8	8.182116	8.368527	8.559332	8.754628	9.159106	9.802114	10.02656	10.49132	10.97799	12.02104	12.57948	13.77566	15.78584	18.08585	8
9	9.228026	9.462213	9.702722	9.949721	10.46388	11.28821	11.57789	12.18079	12.81645	14.19293	14.93742	16.54874	19.30372	22.52131	9
10	10.27917	10.56683	10.86326	11.16872	11.80780	12.84118	13.20679	13.97164	14.78360	16.56029	17.53117	19.65458	23.34928	27.75514	10
11	11.33556	11.68250	12.04121	12.41209	13.19203	14.46403	14.91713	15.86994	16.88845	19.14072	20.38428	23.13313	28.00167	33.93107	11
12	12.39724	12.80933	13.23683	13.68033	14.61779	16.15991	16.71298	17.88214	19.14064	21.95338	23.52271	27.02911	33.35192	41.21866	12
13	13.46423	13.94742	14.45038	14.97394	16.08632	17.93211	18.59863	20.01507	21.55049	25.01919	26.97498	31.39260	39.50471	49.81802	13
14	14.53655	15.09690	15.68214	16.29342	17.59891	19.78405	20.57856	22.27597	24.12902	28.36092	30.77248	36.27971	46.58041	59.96527	14
15	15.61423	16.25786	16.93237	17.63929	19.15688	21.71934	22.65749	24.67253	26.88805	32.00340	34.94973	41.75328	54.71747	71.93901	15
16	16.69730	17.43044	18.20136	19.01207	20.76159	23.74171	24.84037	27.21288	29.84022	35.97370	39.54470	47.88367	64.07509	86.06804	16
17	17.78579	18.61475	19.48938	20.41231	22.41444	25.85508	27.13238	29.90565	32.99903	40.30134	44.59917	54.74971	74.83636	102.7403	17
18	18.87972	19.81090	20.79672	21.84056	24.11687	28.06356	29.53900	32.75999	36.37896	45.01846	50.15909	62.43968	87.21181	122.4135	18
19	19.97912	21.01900	22.12367	23.29737	25.87037	30.37142	32.06595	35.78559	39.99549	50.16012	56.27500	71.05244	101.4436	145.6280	19
20	21.08401	22.23919	23.47052	24.78332	27.67649	32.78314	34.71925	38.99273	43.86518	55.76453	63.00250	80.69874	117.8101	173.0210	20
22	23.31040	24.71630	26.22514	27.84496	31.45288	37.93703	40.43048	45.99583	52.43614	68.53194	78.54302	103.6029	158.2764	243.4868	22
24	25.55912	27.24320	29.06302	31.03030	35.45926	43.56521	46.72710	53.86451	62.24904	83.70090	97.34706	132.3339	211.7930	341.6035	24
26	27.83037	29.82089	31.98668	34.34432	39.70963	49.71132	53.66913	62.70577	73.48382	101.7231	120.0999	168.3740	282.5688	478.2211	26
28	30.12439	32.45039	34.99870	37.79223	44.21885	56.42303	61.32271	72.63980	86.34653	123.1354	147.6309	213.5828	376.1697	668.4475	28
30	32.44142	35.13274	38.10176	41.37944	49.00268	63.75239	69.76079	83.80168	101.0730	148.5752	180.9434	270.2926	499.9569	933.3186	30
36	39.53279	43.50765	47.98511	53.03425	65.17422	90.04134	100.6281	126.2681	159.3374	257.3759	329.0395	542.5987	1166.498	2530.686	36
42	46.83957	52.39778	58.79199	66.15947	84.48389	124.2764	141.9933	186.5076	246.7765	439.8457	591.4007	1080.083	2708.246	6842.865	42
48	54.36832	61.83483	70.60870	80.94059	107.5406	168.8594	197.4267	271.9584	377.9990	745.8656	1056.190	2140.981	6274.405	18483.83	48
54	62.12577	71.85246	83.52960	97.58653	135.0716	226.9180	271.7126	393.1720	574.9286	1259.092	1879.591	4235.005	14523.15	49909.23	54
60	70.11888	82.48637	97.65787	116.3326	167.9450	302.5254	371.2629	565.1159	870.4668	2119.823	3338.298	8368.238	33602.99	134743.8	60

Notes

Notes